Christian Traits for Kids

By

Tracy Carol Taylor

Christian Traits For Kids

Copyright © 2025 by Tracy Carol Taylor. All Rights Reserved.

_____

No part of this publication may be reproduced, stored in a retrieval system, or transmitted in any way by any means, electronic, mechanical, photocopy, recording, or otherwise, without the proper permission of the author except as provided by USA copyright law.

The Lockman Foundation takes scripture quotations marked (AMP) from the Amplified Bible, Copyright © 1954, 1958, 1962, 1964, 1965, 1987 by The Lockman Foundation. Used by permission.

Scripture quotations marked (KJV) are taken from the Holy Bible, King James Version, Cambridge, 1769, and used by permission. All rights reserved.

Scripture quotations marked (NIV) are taken from the Holy Bible, New International Version, NIV, Copyright © 1973, 1978, 1984 by Biblica, Inc. ™ Used by permission of Zondervan. All rights reserved worldwide. www.zondervan.com

The opinions expressed by the author are not necessarily those of Prince of Pages, Inc.

_____

Published by Prince of Pages, Inc.
N. Carlin Springs Road | Arlington, VA 22203 USA

www.princeofpages.com

Cover design by Midjourney

Published in the United States of America

ISBN: 978-1-949252-52-1

1. Religion, Christian Life, Devotional
2. Religion, Christian Life, Personal Growth

Table of Contents

Introduction	**7**
Chapter 1	10
Chapter 2	13
Chapter 3	16
Chapter 4	19
Chapter 5	22
Chapter 6	26
Chapter 7	29
Chapter 8	32
Chapter 9	35
Chapter 10	38
Chapter 11	41
Chapter 12	44
Chapter 13	47

Chapter 14	50
Chapter 15	53
Chapter 16	56
Chapter 17	59
Chapter 18	62
Chapter 19	66
Chapter 20	69
Chapter 21	73
Chapter 22	77
Chapter 23	80
Chapter 24	83
Chapter 25	87
Chapter 26	91
Chapter 27	94
Chapter 28	98
Chapter 29	102

Chapter 30	**106**
Chapter 31	**109**
Chapter 32	**113**
Chapter 33	**116**
Chapter 34	**120**
Chapter 35	**124**
Chapter 36	**128**
Chapter 37	**132**
Chapter 38	**136**
Chapter 39	**140**
Chapter 40	**144**
Chapter 41	**148**
Chapter 42	**152**
Chapter 43	**156**
Chapter 44	**160**
Chapter 45	**164**

Chapter 46	**168**
Chapter 47	**172**
Chapter 48	**176**
Chapter 49	**180**
Chapter 50	**184**
Chapter 51	**188**
Chapter 52	**192**
Chapter 53	**196**
Chapter 54	**200**
Chapter 55	**203**
Chapter 56	**206**
Chapter 57	**209**
Chapter 58	**213**
Chapter 59	**216**
Chapter 60	**220**

Introduction

Building Blocks of Character

What is this book about?

This book is about good character traits that help us grow strong and kind. It teaches us that what we put into our minds and hearts matters, just like what we put into our bodies!

Main Ideas

Just like a computer needs good information to work well ("Garbage In, Garbage Out"), our minds need good thoughts and ideas. What we watch, listen to, and learn shapes who we become.

This book shares Sixty Christian traits that are like building blocks for being a good person. Each one has:

A simple definition

A Bible verse to remember

A story from the Bible that shows the trait

Ideas for how to use it in your life

Did You Know?

Just like plants need good soil, water, and sunlight to grow strong, people need good values, love, and wisdom to grow into their best selves!

Try This!

Make a "Character Growth Chart" on your wall. Each time you practice one of the good traits from this book (like being kind, truthful, or brave), add a sticker or mark on your chart. Watch how much you can grow!

Ways to build good character:

Choose shows and music with positive messages

Spend time with people who are kind and helpful

Practice one new good trait each week

Talk about the good choices characters make in stories

Prayer: "Dear God, help me fill my mind and heart with good things. Thank you for giving us your Word to teach us how to live. Please help me and my family grow strong in good character. Amen."

Remember: "Finally, brethren, whatsoever things are true, whatsoever things are honest, whatsoever things are just, whatsoever things are pure, whatsoever things are lovely, whatsoever things are of good report; if there be any virtue, and if there be any praise, think on these things."

- Philippians 4:8

Chapter 1

Attentive: Being a Good Listener

Good listeners use their ears more than their mouths. They pay careful attention when others speak, which makes God happy!

Bible Story: The Lord Calls Samuel

1 Samuel 3:1-10

Samuel was a young boy who helped in God's temple. One night while sleeping, Samuel heard someone call his name.

He jumped up and ran to Eli, the old priest, saying, "Here I am! You called me!"

Eli said, "I didn't call you. Go back to bed."

This happened two more times!

Finally, Eli realized God was calling Samuel. He told Samuel, "Next time you hear the voice, say 'Speak, Lord, for your servant is listening.'"

When God called again, "Samuel! Samuel!" the boy answered, "Speak, for your servant is listening."

Because Samuel listened well, God gave him an important message.

Did You Know? God gave you two ears but only one mouth! That might be because He wants you to listen twice as much as you talk.

Try This: The next time your teacher or parent is talking, try these listening steps:

Look at their face.

Keep your body still.

Think about what they're saying.

Wait until they finish before you talk.

Prayer: "Dear God, help me be a good listener like Samuel. Help me listen to my parents, my teachers, and most of all, to you. Amen."

Remember: When you talk all the time, you might miss something important! Good listeners learn more and make others feel special.

Chapter 2

Available: Being Ready to Help

Being ready to help means saying "Yes!" when someone needs you. It means sharing what you have with others.

Bible Story: The Boy with the Lunch of Fishes and Loaves

John 6:8-13

A large crowd came to hear Jesus teach. After a long day, everyone was hungry. But they were far from any stores where they could buy food.

Jesus wanted to feed all the people. His helper, Andrew, found a young boy who had brought a lunch. He had just five small loaves of bread and two little fish.

"May we have your lunch to feed people?" Andrew asked the boy.

The boy could have said, "No! This is MY lunch!" Instead, he happily gave his lunch to Jesus.

Jesus thanked God for the food and shared it with everyone. Guess what? That small lunch fed over 5,000 people! They even had twelve baskets of leftovers.

The boy was ready to help when asked. Because he shared, he saw Jesus perform an amazing miracle!

Did You Know? When you share what you have, God can use it to do big things!

Try This:

Ask your mom or dad: "How can I help you today?"

Share your toys with friends or siblings.

When someone asks for help, smile and say, "I'd be happy to!"

Prayer: "Dear Jesus, help me be ready to share and help others. Use me to do good things for people. Amen."

Remember: When you're ready to help, you could be part of something amazing that God is doing!

Chapter 3

Committed: Keeping Your Promise to God

Being Committed means following Him even when it's hard. It means trusting God to lead you the right way.

Bible Story: The Calling of the First Disciples

Mark 1:16-20 and Matthew 9:9

One day, Jesus was walking by a lake. He saw some men fishing. Their names were Simon, Andrew, James, and John. They were catching fish to sell.

Jesus said to them, "Come, follow me. I will make you fishers of people!"

Do you know what the fishermen did? They didn't say, "Maybe later" or "Let me think about it." They put down their fishing nets RIGHT AWAY and followed Jesus!

Later, Jesus saw a man named Matthew collecting money at his booth. Jesus said, "Follow me." Matthew immediately stood up, left his job, and followed Jesus.

These men made a promise to follow Jesus, and they kept it! They trusted Jesus to lead them, and He did.

Did You Know? When you keep promises to God, He helps you do amazing things!

Try This:

Make a small promise like "I will read one Bible story before bed."

Write it down on a piece of paper.

Put a check mark on the paper each day you keep your promise.

See how many days in a row you can keep your promise!

Prayer: "Dear Jesus, help me follow you like the disciples did. Please help me keep my promises to you. I trust you to lead me. Amen."

Remember: Start with small promises. As you keep them, then you can make bigger ones. God loves it when we trust Him!

Chapter 4

Compassionate: Being Kind and Caring

Being Compassionate means loving others when they are sad or need help and doing something to make them feel better.

Bible Story: The Good Samaritan

Luke 10:25-37

Jesus once told a story about a man who was walking on a road. Some bad men hurt him, took his clothes, and left him on the ground. He was very hurt!

Three people walked by:

A priest saw the hurt man but walked on the other side of the road.

Another important man also saw him but kept walking.

Then a Samaritan man (someone people didn't like much) came by.

The Samaritan stopped right away! He cleaned the hurt man's cuts, put him on his donkey, and took him to a hotel. The Samaritan even paid the hotel owner to take care of the hurt man until he got better.

Jesus asked, "Who was a good neighbor to the hurt man?"

The answer was, "The one who showed kindness."

Jesus said, "Go and do the same!"

Did You Know? When you help someone else, it makes YOU feel good too!

Try This:

Look for someone who needs help today.

Ask if you can help them.

Watch how happy they become when you show you care.

Remember how good it feels to be kind!

Prayer: "Dear Jesus, help me notice when people are sad or need help. Give me a caring heart like the Good Samaritan. Amen."

Remember: Everyone needs kindness sometimes. When you help others, they might help someone else too, and kindness spreads all around!

Chapter 5

Confident: Standing Tall

Having a strong belief in what I say and do will benefit me and others, knowing that God is with me.

Bible Story: David Fights Goliath

1 Samuel 17:1-58

There was a boy named David who took care of sheep. One day, David's father sent him to bring food to his older brothers, who were soldiers.

When David arrived at the army camp, he saw something scary. A GIANT man named Goliath was yelling at the Israelite army. Goliath was over nine feet tall (that's taller than a door)! He wore heavy metal armor and carried huge weapons.

Every day, Goliath shouted, "Send one man to fight me! If he wins, we'll be your servants. If I win, you'll be our servants!" All the soldiers were too scared to fight him.

But David wasn't scared! He told King Saul, "I'll fight this giant!"

The king said, "You're too young and small!"

David replied, "When I watch my father's sheep, I've fought lions and bears to protect them. God helped me then, and God will help me now!"

David didn't wear heavy armor. He just took his sling and five smooth stones from a stream. When Goliath saw little David, he laughed.

David called out, "You come with weapons, but I come with God's help!"

David put one stone in his sling, whirled it around, and let it fly. The stone hit Goliath right in the forehead, and the giant fell down!

David wasn't afraid because he knew God was with him.

Did You Know? You don't have to be big or strong to do great things. God can help you do amazing things if you believe!

Try This:

Think of something that scares you.

Draw a picture of yourself being brave.

Write on your picture: "I can do all things through Christ who gives me strength!"

When you feel scared, look at your picture and remember God is with you.

Prayer: "Dear God, help me be brave like David. When I feel scared, help me remember You are with me. Thank you for making me special just the way I am. Amen."

Remember: Being brave doesn't mean never feeling scared. It means trusting God to help you even when you are scared!

Chapter 6

Consistent: Doing the Right Thing Every Day

Being Consistent means making good choices all the time and every day, not just sometimes.

Bible Story: Daniel is Consistent in All His Ways

Daniel 6:1-28

There was a man named Daniel who loved God very much. Daniel lived in a king's palace far from his home.

King Darius liked Daniel because Daniel always did his work well and never told lies. The king made Daniel one of the kingdom's top three helpers!

Some other helpers were jealous of Daniel. They knew Daniel prayed to God three times every day. So, they tricked the king into making a new rule: "For thirty days, no one can pray to any god. They may only pray to the king. Anyone who breaks this rule will be thrown into a lion's den!"

When Daniel heard about the new rule, what do you think he did? He kept praying to God, just like always! He opened his window and got on his knees to pray three times that day, just like he always did.

The jealous men saw Daniel praying and told the king. The king was very sad because he liked Daniel, but had to follow his own rule. Daniel was thrown into a den of lions!

The king couldn't sleep all night. Early the next morning, he ran to the lions' den and called, "Daniel, was your God able to save you from the lions?"

Daniel answered, "My God sent an angel to shut the lions' mouths! They haven't hurt me at all!"

The king was so happy! Daniel was saved because he kept doing the right thing every day, even when it was hard.

Did You Know? When you do the right thing every day, people learn they can trust you!

Try This:

Pick ONE good habit to do every day (like making your bed or saying "please" and "thank you").

Do this SAME good thing EVERY day for a whole week.

Ask a grown-up to help you remember.

Prayer: "Dear God, help me to be like Daniel and do the right thing every day, even when it's hard. Help me be someone people can trust. Amen."

Remember: God is happy when we do the right thing all the time, not just when it's easy!

Chapter 7

Content: Being Happy With What You Have

Being Content means saying "Thank you, God," for your toys, home, and family instead of always wanting more.

Bible Story: Esau Greets His Brother Jacob

Genesis 33:1-9

In the Bible, there were two brothers named Jacob and Esau who hadn't seen each other for many years. Jacob was afraid because he and Esau had fought before he moved away.

When Jacob heard Esau was coming with 400 men, he was very scared! Jacob sent many animals as gifts to Esau, hoping his brother wouldn't be angry.

But when they finally met, something wonderful happened! Esau ran to Jacob and gave him a big hug. They were both so happy that they cried!

Jacob tried to give Esau many gifts. But Esau smiled and said something very wise: "I have plenty, my brother; keep what you have for yourself."

Esau wasn't greedy. He was happy with what he already had. He didn't need more animals or things to be happy.

Did You Know? The Bible says, "We brought nothing into this world, and we can take nothing out." That means the most important things aren't toys or games!

Try This:

Look around your room and count FIVE things you're thankful for.

Say "Thank you, God," for each one.

Make a "Happy With What I Have" list and draw pictures of things you already have that make you smile.

When you want something new, first think about the good things you already have.

Prayer: "Dear God, help me be like Esau and say, 'I have plenty.' Thank you for all the things you've given me. Help me be happy with what I have. Amen."

Remember: Having more toys doesn't make you happier! Being thankful for what you have brings real happiness.

Chapter 8

Cooperative: Working Together

Being cooperative means helping each other instead of doing everything by yourself. When we work as a team, we can do amazing things!

Bible Story: The First Christians and Their Fellowship

Acts 2:42-47

After Jesus went back to heaven, His followers (called the apostles) taught many people about Him, and more and more people believed in Him.

All these new Christians became like a big family! Here's what they did:

They met together every day to learn and pray.

They shared their food with each other.

If someone didn't have enough, others would help them.

They ate meals together in each other's homes.

They were happy and thankful.

Everyone worked together and shared what they had.

No one said, "That's MINE!" or "I don't WANT to!" Because they worked together so well, more people wanted to join them every day!

Did You Know? A single stick can break easily, but bundling many sticks together makes them very strong!

Try This:

Help clean up your room with your family - everyone pick up something!

Play a game where everyone has a job (like building a fort or baking cookies).

Make a "Helper Chart" with chores you can do to help at home.

Next time someone asks for your help, say "Yes!" with a smile.

Prayer: "Dear God, help me be a good helper. Show me how to work well with others without arguing. Help me share and be kind. Amen."

Remember: When we all do our part, like puzzle pieces fitting together, we can do BIG things that one person could never do alone!

Chapter 9

Courageous: Being Brave

Realizing that God has given me the mental and moral strength to face and withstand any danger, fear, trial, or difficulty.

Bible Story: David Fights Lions and Bears
1 Samuel 17:33-36

David was a young boy who took care of his father's sheep. This was an important job! David had to keep the sheep safe from dangerous animals.

One day, a lion came and grabbed one of the sheep. Another time, a bear tried to take a sheep. Most people would run away from lions and bears because they're so scary!

But David wasn't just any shepherd boy. He knew God was with him. Instead of running away, David chased after these wild animals! He fought the lion and the bear, and he saved the sheep.

Later, when David needed to fight the giant Goliath, King Saul said, "You can't fight him! You're just a boy!"

David answered, "I protected my sheep from lions and bears. God helped me then, and God will help me now!"

David was brave because he trusted God to be with him when things were scary.

Did You Know? Everyone feels scared sometimes - even grown-ups! Being brave doesn't mean never feeling afraid. Being courageous means doing what's right even when you are afraid.

Try This:

Draw a picture of something that makes you feel scared.

Ask a grown-up to help you write on your picture: "God is with me!"

When you feel afraid, remember David and how God helped him be brave.

Say this when you're scared: "God, please help me be courageous!"

Prayer: "Dear God, sometimes I feel afraid. Please help me be brave like David. Thank you for always being with me, even when scary things happen. Amen."

Remember: God promises, "I will never leave you or forsake you." That means God is ALWAYS with you, helping you be courageous!

Chapter 10

Creative: Using Your Special Gifts

Being Creative means using your special gifts means finding the talents God gave you and using them to help others and make God happy.

Bible Story: David Plays His Harp for King Saul

1 Samuel 16: 17-23

King Saul was having a hard time. He felt sad and upset a lot. He needed someone who could play beautiful music to help him feel better.

One of his helpers said, "I know a boy named David who plays the harp beautifully! He's a shepherd boy who takes care of his father's sheep."

So, King Saul sent for David. When David came to the palace, he brought his harp with him. Whenever King Saul felt sad or upset, David would play his harp. The beautiful music helped the king feel peaceful and happy again.

David used his special gift of music to help someone who was sad. God had given David this talent, and David used it to make someone else's life better.

Did You Know? God gives EVERYONE special gifts and talents! Some people can sing, some can draw, some can build things, and some are good at making friends. What special gifts has God given YOU?

Try This:

Think about things you enjoy doing (like drawing, singing, building, or helping).

Try something new this week - maybe a new craft or game.

Use your talent to make someone happy (draw a picture for Grandma, help Mom bake cookies, or sing a song for a friend who's sad).

Thank God for giving you special gifts.

Prayer: "Dear God, thank you for the special gifts and talents you've given me. Help me use them to make others happy and to show your love. Amen."

Remember: When we use our talents to help others, we show God's love in a special way that only WE can do!

Chapter 11

Decisive: Making Good Choices

Being Decisive means doing what God wants, even when others are doing something different.

Bible Story: Daniel in Captivity

Daniel 1:3-5 and Daniel 1:8-16

Daniel was a young boy who was taken far from his home to live in a king's palace in Babylon. The king wanted Daniel and his friends to learn the Babylonian language and customs.

The king gave them rich food and wine from his own table. This food looked delicious! But Daniel knew something important - some of this food wasn't allowed by God's rules.

Daniel had a big choice to make. Should he eat the king's food like everyone else? Or should he follow God's rules?

Daniel made a firm decision. He would NOT eat the king's food.

Instead, he politely asked the guard, "Please give us just vegetables and water for ten days. Then see if we look healthier than the others."

The guard was worried but agreed to try. After ten days, Daniel and his friends looked healthier and stronger than all the other young men!

Because Daniel decided to follow God's rules, God blessed him. Daniel stood firm in his decision, even when it wasn't the easy choice.

Did You Know? The small choices you make every day can lead to big things! Each time you choose to do what's right, it gets easier the next time.

Try This:

When someone wants you to do something wrong, say "No, thank you" in a kind but firm voice.

Before making a choice, ask yourself, "What would God want me to do?"

Practice making good choices in small things (like picking up toys without being asked).

Thank God when He helps you make good choices.

Prayer: "Dear God, help me make good choices like Daniel did. When others try to get me to do wrong things, help me be strong and do what's right. Amen."

Remember: You can decide to do what's right, even when everyone else is doing something different!

Chapter 12

Dependable: Being Someone Others Can Count On

Being Dependable means doing what you say you will do. It means being a helper whom people can trust.

Bible Story: The Calling of Elisha

1 Kings 19:19-21 and 2 Kings 2:1-2

There was a prophet named Elijah who worked for God. One day, God told Elijah to find a helper named Elisha.

Elisha was working hard in his field with twelve pairs of oxen when Elijah came to him. Elijah put his cloak around Elisha's shoulders, which was a special way of saying, "God wants you to help me now."

Elisha understood right away. He said goodbye to his parents, then did something surprising - he cooked his oxen and gave a big farewell meal to everyone! This showed he was completely ready to follow Elijah.

From that day on, Elisha helped Elijah with everything. He was always there when Elijah needed him.

Later, when Elijah was about to be taken up to heaven, he told Elisha, "You can stay here."

But Elisha said, "I will not leave you!" He was determined to stay with Elijah until the very end.

Elisha was someone Elijah could always count on. He was dependable.

Did You Know? When people know they can count on you, they trust you with more important jobs!

Try This:

When you tell Mom or Dad you'll do something, do it right away.

Take care of your responsibilities without being reminded (like feeding a pet or putting away toys).

If you promise to meet a friend, be on time.

Finish what you start - don't leave jobs half-done.

Prayer: "Dear God, help me be dependable like Elisha. Help me keep my promises and do my best job at everything. Help me be someone others can count on. Amen."

Remember: Being dependable means people can trust you. When you say you'll do something, do it completely and do it well!

Chapter 13

Determination: Not Giving Up

Determination means trying hard even when things get tough. It means finishing what you start.

Bible Story: Nehemiah Rebuilds the Walls of Jerusalem

Nehemiah 2:13-18

Nehemiah loved God and God's people. One day, he heard that the walls around Jerusalem had been broken down. This made him very sad because, without walls, the city wasn't safe.

Nehemiah decided to rebuild those walls! This was a huge job that would take lots of people and hard work.

First, Nehemiah went to look at all the broken walls at night. He didn't tell anyone what he was planning. He carefully checked every part of the wall to understand how big the job would be.

Then Nehemiah told the people, "Look at our city! The walls are broken, and the gates are burned. Let's rebuild them together!"

Nehemiah also told them how God was helping him. The people got excited and said, "Yes! Let's start rebuilding!"

The job wasn't easy. Some people made fun of them. Some people tried to stop them. But Nehemiah didn't give up! He kept working and encouraging others until the walls were finished.

Because Nehemiah was determined, the whole city became safe again.

Did You Know? Many great things were invented by people who failed many times but didn't give up! The Wright brothers crashed their flying machines many times before they finally flew!

Try This:

Think of something hard you want to finish (like learning to tie your shoes or ride a bike).

Break it into small steps so it's not so scary.

Keep trying even if you make mistakes.

When you feel like quitting, say, "I can do this with God's help!"

Prayer: "Dear God, help me not give up when things get hard. Help me be determined like Nehemiah. I know with your help, I can finish what I start. Amen."

Remember: God loves it when we try our hardest and don't give up! With God's help, you can do hard things!

Chapter 14

Devotion: Loving God First

Devotion means making God the most important person in your life and putting him first. It means showing God you love Him every day.

Bible Story: God Calls Abraham

Genesis 12:1-7

God spoke to a man named Abram (later called Abraham). God told him, "Leave your home, your family, and everything familiar. Go to a new land that I will show you."

This was a big ask! God wanted Abram to leave everything he knew and loved—his house, his friends, his favorite places. Abram was 75 years old. He was not a young man anymore!

Did Abram say, "That's too hard" or "Maybe later"? No! The Bible says, "So Abram left, as the LORD had told him." He packed up everything he owned. He took his wife Sarai, his nephew Lot, and all their animals and servants.

Abram didn't even know exactly where he was going! He just knew God wanted him to go, so he went. That's how much Abram loved and trusted God.

When Abram finally arrived in the new land called Canaan, the first thing he did was build an altar to thank God. This showed that God was still first in Abram's heart even in a new place.

Did You Know? When you love someone, you want to spend time with them! One way to show God you love Him is by spending time with Him each day.

Try This:

Start each day by saying "Good morning, God!"

Look at a Bible storybook before bedtime.

Thank God for three things every day.

When you hear about something fun to do, first ask if it helps you love God better.

Prayer: "Dear God, help me love You most of all. Like Abraham, help me follow You even when it's hard. I want to put you first in everything I do. Amen."

Remember: When we love God first, He promises to bless us and guide us, just like He did for Abraham!

Chapter 15

Diligent: Working Hard at Everything

Working hard at everything means doing your best job, even when the job isn't fun. It means working cheerfully and carefully.

Bible Story: Joseph in Potiphar's House
Genesis 39:1-6

Joseph was a young man who had a very hard time. His own brothers were so jealous of him that they sold him as a slave! Joseph was taken far away to Egypt, where he didn't know anyone and couldn't even speak the language well.

He was bought by a man named Potiphar, who was an important officer in Egypt.

Joseph could have been angry and done a bad job. He could have thought, "Why should I work hard? I'm just a slave!"

But Joseph didn't do that. Instead, he worked very, very hard at everything Potiphar asked him to do. He was careful and attentive and always did his best work.

Potiphar noticed how hard Joseph worked. He saw that everything Joseph did turned out well because God was helping him. Potiphar was so impressed that he put Joseph in charge of his whole house and everything he owned!

Even though Joseph was still a slave, his situation got much better because of his hard work. God blessed Joseph because he did his best even in a hard situation.

Did You Know? When you work hard and do your best, God notices - even if no one else does!

Try This:

Pick one chore you don't like doing and try to do it extra well today.

Don't complain while doing your work.

Finish a job completely instead of leaving it half-done.

Remember you're working for God, not just for people.

Prayer: "Dear God, help me work hard like Joseph, even when I don't feel like it. Help me remember that when I do my best, I'm showing my love for you. Amen."

Remember: God is happy when you work hard and do your best job at everything - schoolwork, chores, or helping others. Your hard work honors God!

Chapter 16

Discreet: Keeping Secrets Safe

Keeping secrets safe means not telling things that might hurt someone's feelings or embarrass them. It means being someone others can trust.

Bible Story: Mary and Joseph

Matthew 1:18-25

Mary was going to marry Joseph. But before they got married, something surprising happened - Mary was going to have a baby! This baby was very special because God put this baby in Mary's tummy. This baby would grow up to be Jesus!

Joseph had a problem. In those days, if a woman was going to have a baby before she got married, people would be very unkind to her. They might even throw stones at her!

Joseph loved Mary and didn't want people to be mean to her. The Bible says Joseph was a good man who "did not want to expose her to public disgrace." This means he didn't want to tell everyone and make Mary feel ashamed.

Joseph decided he would quietly break off the wedding without telling everyone why. This was being discreet - keeping Mary's situation private to protect her.

Then an angel came to Joseph in a dream and told him the baby was from God. Joseph decided to marry Mary after all, still keeping the secret of how special this baby really was.

Joseph was discreet about Mary's situation, and this helped keep baby Jesus safe.

Did You Know? Being discreet means thinking before you speak and keeping private things private.

Try This:

If you see someone do something embarrassing, don't tell others about it.

If a friend tells you a secret, keep it safe.

When someone looks different or makes a mistake, please don't point it out to everyone.

Practice saying, "That's private" when someone asks you to tell a secret.

Prayer: "Dear God, help me be like Joseph and keep secrets safe. Help me think before I speak, and never hurt someone by telling their private business. Amen."

Remember: People who keep secrets safe have more friends because others know they can be trusted!

Chapter 17

Efficient: Using Time and Talents Wisely

Using time and talents wisely means finding the best way to do things without wasting time or making mistakes.

Bible Story: The Shrewd Servant

Luke 16:1-8

Jesus told a story about a manager who worked for a rich man. One day, the rich man heard that his manager was wasting his money. He told the manager, "I want to see all your accounts. I think I'll have to fire you!"

The manager thought quickly. "What will I do if I lose my job? I'm not strong enough to dig ditches, and I'm too proud to beg."

He had an idea! He called in people who owed money to his master. To the first one, he said, "How much do you owe?" The man said, "One hundred barrels of oil." The manager said, "Quick! Change your bill to fifty!"

To another who owed one hundred bushels of wheat, he said, "Change your bill to eighty!"

When the rich man found out what his manager had done, he was surprised. Even though the manager hadn't been honest, he was smart about planning for his future. He used his time wisely to solve his problem.

Jesus told this story to teach us about using our time and abilities in the smartest way.

Did You Know? Planning before you start a job can save you lots of time and help you do better work!

Try This:

Make a "To Do" list of things you need to finish today.

Think about the best order to do your chores (like picking up toys before vacuuming).

Gather all your supplies before starting a project.

Ask yourself: "Is there a faster or better way to do this?"

Prayer: "Dear God, help me use my time and talents wisely. Show me how to plan my work and do things right the first time. Help me not waste the gifts you've given me. Amen."

Remember: Doing things the smart way means you'll have more time for fun later!

Chapter 18

Fairness: Being Fair to Others

Being fair means treating others the way you want to be treated. It means thinking about how others feel, not just yourself.

Bible Story: David and Abigail
1 Samuel 25:3-35

There was a man named Nabal who had many sheep. David and his men had been kind to Nabal's shepherds - they had protected them and their sheep from danger.

When it came time to shear the sheep (which was like harvest time when people celebrated), David sent some men to ask Nabal for food. David's message was polite: "We've been kind to your shepherds. Please share some of your feast with us."

But Nabal was mean and selfish. He said, "Who is David? Why should I give MY food to people I don't know?" He sent David's men away with nothing, even though David had helped protect his sheep!

When David heard this, he was so angry that he decided to attack Nabal and his household!

Nabal's wife, Abigail, heard what happened. She was wise and fair. She quickly gathered food - bread, wine, sheep meat, raisins, and figs - and went to meet David.

Abigail apologized for her husband's rudeness. She said, "Please don't do something you'll regret later. Let me give you this food instead."

David saw she was being fair and changed his mind about attacking. He said, "Thank you for stopping me from doing something I would have regretted."

Abigail saved many lives because she was fair and saw both sides of the situation.

Did You Know? Being fair means thinking about what's right, not just what you want.

Try This:

When playing games, take turns and follow the rules.

Share your toys and treats evenly with friends and siblings.

Listen to both sides of a story before deciding who's right.

Think about how you would feel if someone treated you the way you're treating them.

Prayer: "Dear God, help me be fair like Abigail. Help me think about others' feelings and treat everyone the way I want to be treated. Amen."

Remember: Jesus taught us to "Do to others what you would want them to do to you." ~ Matthew 7:12 This is called the Golden Rule!

Chapter 19

Faithful: Being Loyal and True

Being loyal, dependable, and true to your word, work, and others.

Bible Story: The Parable of the Talents

Matthew 25:14-21

Jesus told a story about a rich man who was going on a long trip. Before he left, he called three servants and gave each some money to take care of while he was gone.

To the first servant, he gave five bags of gold. To the second servant, he gave two bags of gold. To the third servant, he gave one bag of gold.

Then the rich man left on his journey.

The first servant worked hard and used the five bags of gold to earn five more bags! The second servant also worked hard and turned his two bags into four bags! But the third servant was afraid. He just dug a hole and buried his one bag of gold.

When the rich man came back, he asked each servant what they had done with his money.

The first servant said, "You gave me five bags of gold, and I've earned five more!" The rich man was very happy and said, "Well done, good and faithful servant! You kept your promise to take care of my money. Now I'll put you in charge of many more things!"

The second servant showed his four bags, and the rich man was happy with him, too.

But the third servant just gave back the one bag he had buried. The rich man was disappointed because this servant hadn't tried at all.

Did You Know? When you keep your promises, people learn they can trust you with bigger and more important things!

Try This:

Make a promise to do one small job today, and make sure you do it.

If you borrow something, return it when you say you will.

When you tell your mom or dad you'll do something, do it without being reminded.

Thank someone who has kept a promise to you.

Prayer: "Dear God, help me be faithful and keep my promises. Help me be someone others can trust. Thank you for always keeping your promises to me. Amen."

Remember: Just like a building needs a solid foundation to stand strong, your friendships need the solid foundation of faithfulness and trust!

Chapter 20

Fearless: Being Brave with God's Help

Being brave with God's help means not being afraid because you know God is with you, even when things look scary.

Bible Story: Gideon Goes into Battle with God

Judges 6:11-16, Judges 6:33-35, and Judges 7:19-21

There was a man named Gideon who was hiding from his enemies, the Midianites. He was so scared that he was working in a winepress instead of out in the open field where people might see him.

Suddenly, an angel appeared and said something surprising: "The Lord is with you, mighty warrior!"

Gideon was confused. He didn't feel like a mighty warrior at all! He said, "If God is with us, why are we having so many problems? I'm not important - my family is the weakest in our tribe!"

The angel replied, "God will be with you, and you will defeat the Midianites."

Later, God told Gideon to gather an army. But then God did something surprising - He kept making Gideon's army smaller! First, God sent home all the scared soldiers. Then he sent home all but 300 men. Gideon would fight thousands of enemies with just 300 men!

What weapons did they use? Just trumpets, clay jars, and torches! When they surrounded the enemy camp, they blew their trumpets, smashed their jars, and held up their torches, shouting, "A sword for the Lord and for Gideon!"

The enemy soldiers were so confused and frightened that they ran away!

Gideon won because God was with him, even though he started out feeling afraid.

Did You Know? Even heroes in the Bible felt scared sometimes! Being brave doesn't mean never feeling afraid - it means trusting God even when you do feel afraid.

Try This:

When you feel scared, say out loud: "God is with me!"

Draw a picture of something that makes you afraid, then draw God with you in the picture.

Think of a brave Bible hero (like Gideon) when you face something scary.

Remember a time God helped you before when you were afraid.

Prayer: "Dear God, sometimes I feel afraid like Gideon did. Help me remember, you are always with me. Please give me your strength to be brave. Thank you for never leaving me alone. Amen."

Remember: God promised, "I will be with you." That means you're never alone, no matter how scary things seem!

Chapter 21

Forgiving: Forgiving Others

Forgiving means letting go of angry feelings when someone hurts you and giving someone a fresh start.

Bible Story: The Stoning of Stephen

Acts 6:8-14 and Acts 7:54-60

Stephen was a man who loved Jesus very much. He told many people about Jesus and even did miracles to show God's power.

But some people didn't like what Stephen was saying. They became very angry at him. They told lies about him, saying he said bad things about God and Moses, but Stephen hadn't done anything wrong.

These angry people dragged Stephen to court. They had people tell more lies about him. Stephen wasn't scared - he just told the truth about Jesus.

The people became so angry that they took Stephen outside the city and began throwing big stones at him to hurt him. This is called stoning, and it was very painful.

Even while the stones were hitting him and he was dying, Stephen looked up to heaven and saw Jesus. Instead of being angry or asking God to punish these people, Stephen prayed something amazing.

He said, "Lord, do not hold this sin against them." This means Stephen was asking God to forgive the very people who were hurting him!

Stephen forgave the people who were being mean to him, just like Jesus forgave the people who put Him on the cross.

Did You Know? Holding onto angry feelings when someone hurts you is like carrying a heavy backpack full of rocks. When you forgive, it's like putting down that heavy backpack!

Try This:

Think of someone who made you feel sad or angry.

Draw a picture of your angry feelings, then crumple it up and throw it away.

Tell God how you feel and ask Him to help you forgive.

Say to yourself, "I choose to forgive (person's name)".

Prayer: "Dear God, sometimes it's hard to forgive people who hurt my feelings. Help me forgive others just like Stephen did. Thank you for forgiving me when I do wrong things. Amen."

Remember: Jesus taught us to pray, "Forgive us our sins, as we forgive those who sin against us." ~ Matthew 6:9-13 When we forgive others, we're being just like Jesus!

Chapter 22

Friendly: Being a Good Friend

Being a good friend means being kind, helpful, and loyal to others. Good friends stick together through happy and hard times.

Bible Story: Jonathan and David

1 Samuel 18:1-4, 1 Samuel 19:1-7, and 1 Samuel 20:42

King Saul had a son named Jonathan. One day, a young shepherd boy named David came to their palace. Jonathan and David quickly became best friends.

The Bible says Jonathan loved David as much as he loved himself! That's a lot of love! Jonathan even gave David his royal robe, sword, bow, and belt as special gifts to show their friendship.

Later, something sad happened. King Saul became very jealous of David and wanted to hurt him. This put Jonathan in a hard position. Should he be loyal to his father, the king, or to his friend David?

Jonathan chose to be a true friend. He warned David about his father's plan, saying, "My father wants to kill you. Hide tomorrow, and I'll talk to him about you."

Jonathan bravely spoke to his father about David: "David hasn't done anything wrong. He even risked his life to help our kingdom when he fought Goliath!"

Jonathan's kind words worked, and King Saul promised not to hurt David. Jonathan hurried to tell David the good news.

Jonathan and David promised to always be friends, no matter what happened. Jonathan was willing to stand up for his friend, even when it was hard.

Did You Know? The Bible says if you want to have friends, you need to be friendly first!

Try This:

Smile and say hello to someone new at school.

Share your toys or snacks with others.

Say something nice to make someone feel good.

Stand up for a friend if others are being unkind.

Keep the promises you make to your friends.

Prayer: "Dear God, help me be a good friend like Jonathan. Help me be kind, loyal, and helpful to others. Thank you for being my forever friend. Amen."

Remember: Jesus is the best friend of all! He said, "Greater love has no one than this: to lay down one's life for one's friends." Jesus loves us so much He gave His life for us!

Chapter 23

Generous: Sharing with Others

Sharing with others means freely giving of what you have—your toys, your time, or your help. God loves it when we share!

Bible Story: Contributions for Worship

2 Chronicles 31:2-8

Long ago, there was a good king named Hezekiah who loved God very much. He wanted to make sure the priests and Levites (the people who worked in God's temple) had everything they needed to do their jobs.

So, King Hezekiah did two important things:

He gave from his own things for the offerings to God.

He asked the people to share part of their food and animals with the priests.

When the people heard the king's request, something amazing happened! They didn't just give a little - they gave LOTS! They brought the first and best parts of their grain, grapes for wine, olive oil, honey, and everything else they grew. They also brought many of their sheep, cows, and other animals.

The people brought so much that they had to pile it in big heaps! It took them four whole months to bring all their gifts. When King Hezekiah saw these huge piles of gifts, he was so happy that he praised God and blessed the people.

The people were generous because they loved God and wanted to help His workers. Their generosity made everyone happy!

Did You Know? When you share with others, God promises to bless you! The Bible says, "God loves a cheerful giver."

Try This:

Share your favorite toy with a friend or sibling today.

Give some of your snack to someone who doesn't have one.

Help someone with a chore without being asked.

Find a toy you don't use much and give it to someone who would enjoy it.

Save part of your allowance to put in the church offering.

Prayer: "Dear God, You have given me so many good things. Help me share gladly with others. Help me be generous with my toys, my time, and my help. Thank you for teaching me to give. Amen."

Remember: Jesus said, "It is more blessed to give than to receive." This means giving to others makes you happier than getting things for yourself!

Chapter 24

Gentleness: Being Gentle and Kind

Being gentle means being kind, patient, and soft with your words and actions. Gentle people make others feel safe and loved.

Bible Story: Jesus Feeds the Four Thousand

Matthew 15:29-39

One day, Jesus was teaching on a mountain near the Sea of Galilee. Many people came to hear Him. Some were sick or couldn't walk, see, or speak. Jesus healed all of them! The crowd was amazed to see people walking, seeing, and talking who couldn't do these things before.

These people stayed with Jesus for three whole days! They were so interested in what Jesus was teaching that they forgot to bring enough food. Jesus noticed they were hungry.

Jesus called His disciples and said, "I feel sorry for these people. They've been with me for three days and have nothing to eat. I don't want to send them home hungry - they might faint on the way!"

The disciples wondered, "How can we feed so many people way out here in the wilderness?"

Jesus asked gently, "How many loaves of bread do you have?" They answered, "Seven, and a few small fish."

Jesus didn't yell at the people for not bringing food or scold the disciples for not having enough. Instead, He asked everyone to sit down comfortably.

Then Jesus took the bread and fish, thanked God for it, and shared it with everyone. All 4,000 men (plus women and children) ate until they were full! They even had seven baskets of leftovers!

Jesus showed gentleness by caring about people's needs and speaking kindly to them.

Did You Know? The Bible says Jesus is like a shepherd who gently carries little lambs in His arms. That's how He cares for us!

Try This:

Use a soft voice when talking to others.

Pet an animal gently to practice being careful with your hands.

Help someone smaller than you with something they find hard to do.

Say something kind when someone makes a mistake instead of getting upset.

Prayer: "Dear Jesus, help me be gentle like You. Help me use kind words and soft hands. Help me be patient when others make mistakes. Thank you for being gentle with me. Amen."

Remember: A gentle answer turns away anger, but harsh words upset people. Being gentle makes the world a happier place! ~ Proverbs 15:1

Chapter 25

Godliness: Making Good Choices Like God Wants

Making good choices like God wants means doing what is right and staying away from what is wrong. It means becoming more like Jesus every day.

Bible Story: Manasseh Repents

2 Chronicles 33:1-17

A long time ago, there was a boy named Manasseh who became king when he was only 12 years old! But King Manasseh made very bad choices.

Instead of following God like his father had taught him, Manasseh did many wrong things:

He built altars to false gods.

He put idols (statues people worshipped) right in God's temple.

He even hurt his own children as offerings to false gods.

He practiced magic and talked to evil spirits.

God tried to speak to Manasseh, saying, "Please stop doing these wrong things!" But Manasseh wouldn't listen.

Finally, God allowed the king of Assyria to capture Manasseh. Soldiers put hooks in his nose and chains on his arms and took him far away to Babylon as a prisoner. Now, Manasseh wasn't a king anymore - he was a prisoner eating scraps of food!

When things got really bad, Manasseh finally realized he had made terrible mistakes. He prayed to God and said he was sorry for all the wrong things he had done. He asked God to forgive him.

God heard Manasseh's prayer! God forgave him and even brought him back to Jerusalem to be king again. Manasseh was so thankful that he:

Took away all the false gods and idols.

Fixed God's altar in the temple.

Told everyone to worship only the true God.

Manasseh learned that following God's ways leads to a good life, and doing wrong things leads to trouble.

Did You Know? You can always start making good choices, no matter how many wrong choices you've made before. God always gives second chances when we're truly sorry!

Try This:

When you have a choice to make, ask yourself, "What would Jesus do?"

Draw a picture of a road with two paths - one leading to good choices and one to bad choices.

Say "I'm sorry" if you make a wrong choice.

Thank God when He helps you make good choices.

Prayer: "Dear God, help me make good choices like You want me to. When I make mistakes, help me say I'm sorry and change my ways. Thank you for always giving me another chance. Amen."

Remember: God is happiest when we choose to be like Him - kind, honest, and loving!

Chapter 26

Honest: Telling the Truth

Telling the truth means saying and doing what is right, even when it's hard. Honest people can be trusted.

Bible Story: Jesus and Zacchaeus

Luke 19:1-10

There was a man named Zacchaeus who was a tax collector. In those days, tax collectors often took more money than they should and kept the extra for themselves. This made them rich, but people didn't like or trust them.

Zacchaeus was very short and couldn't see over the crowd when Jesus came to town. He wanted to see Jesus so badly that he climbed up in a tree!

When Jesus walked by, He looked up and saw Zacchaeus. Instead of ignoring him like everyone else did, Jesus said, "Zacchaeus, come down! I want to stay at your house today."

Zacchaeus was so excited! He hurried down from the tree. The crowd was surprised and upset. They said, "Why would Jesus visit the home of such a dishonest man?"

But meeting Jesus changed Zacchaeus's heart. He stood up and said, "Lord, I will give half of everything I own to the poor! And if I have cheated anyone, I will pay them back four times as much!"

Jesus was very happy with Zacchaeus's decision to be honest. Jesus said, "Today salvation has come to this house!"

Zacchaeus learned that being honest was better than being rich through cheating.

Did You Know? The Bible says that God loves people who tell the truth and do what is right.

Try This:

Tell the truth even when you might get in trouble.

Return things that don't belong to you.

Do what you say you will do.

If you make a mistake, admit it and try to fix it.

Play games without cheating, even if you really want to win.

Prayer: "Dear God, help me be honest like Zacchaeus became. Help me tell the truth and do what's right, even when it's hard. Thank you for loving me when I make mistakes. Amen."

Remember: It's better to be honest and trusted than to be dishonest and have lots of things. An honest person can sleep peacefully at night!

Chapter 27

Humble: Not Thinking Too Highly of Yourself

Not thinking too highly of yourself means being modest and not acting like you're better than others. It means seeing the good in others instead of just yourself.

Bible Story: Jesus Anointed by a Sinful Woman
Luke 7:36-50

One day, a Pharisee (an important religious leader) named Simon invited Jesus to dinner at his house. This was a special invitation because Pharisees were considered very important people.

During the dinner, something unexpected happened. A woman who had done many wrong things in her life heard that Jesus was at Simon's house. She brought a beautiful jar of expensive perfume.

The woman stood behind Jesus, crying so much that her tears fell on his feet. Then she did something amazing - she knelt down and wiped Jesus' feet with her own hair! Then she kissed his feet and poured her expensive perfume on them.

Simon the Pharisee thought to himself, "If Jesus was really a prophet, he would know what kind of sinful woman is touching him!"

Jesus knew what Simon was thinking. He told Simon a story about two people who owed money - one owed a little and one owed a lot. When both debts were forgiven, Jesus asked which person would be more thankful.

Then Jesus pointed out how humble the woman was compared to Simon. Simon hadn't even offered Jesus water to wash his dusty feet (which was the polite thing to do for guests). But this woman washed his feet with her tears and dried them with her hair!

The woman was humble because she knew she needed forgiveness. Simon was proud and thought he was better than her. Jesus forgave the woman's sins because of her humble heart.

Did You Know? The Bible says God gives special help (called grace) to people who are humble, but He opposes people who are proud!

Try This:

Let someone else go first in a game or in line.

Say "thank you" when someone helps you.

Tell others about the good things they do instead of bragging about yourself.

Practice saying "I'm sorry" when you make a mistake.

Ask for help when you need it instead of pretending you know everything.

Prayer: "Dear God, help me not think I'm better than others. Help me be humble like the woman who washed Jesus' feet. Thank you for loving me even when I make mistakes. Amen."

Remember: Being humble doesn't mean thinking less of yourself - it means thinking of yourself less and thinking of others more!

Chapter 28

Joyful: Being Happy in God

Being happy in God means having joy that comes from knowing God loves you. It means showing your happiness by singing, smiling, and being kind to others.

Bible Story: The Ark is Brought to Jerusalem

1 Chronicles 15:1-4, 1 Chronicles 15:11-16, and 1 Chronicles 15:25-28

King David wanted to bring the special Ark of God to Jerusalem. The Ark was a beautiful gold box that represented God's presence with His people. It was very sacred!

David carefully planned everything. He called the Levites (the special helpers in God's temple) and told them, "You are the ones God chose to carry the Ark. Get yourselves ready for this important job!"

David remembered that the last time they tried to move the Ark, they didn't follow God's instructions, and that caused problems. This time, they would do it exactly right!

The Levites carried the Ark carefully on poles on their shoulders, just as God had told Moses long ago. But David didn't want this to be just a serious, quiet event. He wanted it to be JOYFUL!

David told the leaders to choose singers and musicians to play harps, lyres, and cymbals. He wanted them to sing HAPPY songs as they brought the Ark to Jerusalem!

When the big day came, all Israel celebrated! They shouted with joy, blew trumpets and rams' horns, played music, and sang happy songs. David himself danced with all his might! Everyone was so happy that God's special Ark was coming to Jerusalem.

It was a day full of joy and celebration because God was with His people!

Did You Know? Being joyful can help you feel better when you're sad, and it can help others feel better too!

Try This:

Sing a happy song to God, even if you don't think you have a good voice.

Dance around your room to praise God (like David did!).

Draw a picture of things that make you happy, and thank God for them.

Smile at someone who looks sad today.

Tell a funny joke to make someone laugh.

Prayer: "Dear God, fill my heart with Your joy! Help me be the kind of person who brings happiness when I enter a room. Thank you for all the good things you've given me. Amen."

Remember: The Bible says, "The joy of the Lord is your strength!" ~ Nehemiah 8:10

Being happy because of God's love gives you the strength to face hard days!

Chapter 29

Just: Being Fair and Honest

Being fair and honest means treating others the right way and always telling the truth. It means doing what's right, even when no one is watching.

Bible Story: Abraham Buries Sarah

Genesis 23:3-19

Abraham's wife Sarah had died, and he needed a place to bury her. Abraham was living in a land that wasn't his home country. He was a foreigner among the Hittite people.

Abraham went to speak to the Hittites. He said politely, "I'm a stranger living among you. Please sell me some land so I can bury my wife."

The Hittites respected Abraham and said, "You are an honored prince among us! Take any of our tombs to bury your dead. No one will refuse you."

Abraham bowed to show his thanks and asked specifically about a cave called Machpelah that belonged to a man named Ephron.

When Ephron heard Abraham's request, he said, "No, my lord! I'll GIVE you the field and the cave! You can have it for free. Everyone here is my witness - I'm giving it to you!"

But Abraham didn't want to take the land for free, even though Ephron offered. Abraham insisted on paying the full price—400 pieces of silver. He weighed out the silver in front of everyone at the city gate, where business was done publicly so all could see it was fair.

Abraham was being just and fair. He could have taken the land for free, but he wanted to pay what it was worth so no one could ever say he took advantage of Ephron.

Did You Know? God wants us to use fair weights and measures. In Bible times, that meant having honest scales for weighing goods. Today, it means being fair in all our dealings with others!

Try This:

Use the same rules for everyone when playing games.

Return extra change if a store clerk gives you too much money.

Tell the truth, even when it would be easier to tell a lie.

Treat others the way you want to be treated.

Share things equally when dividing with friends or siblings.

Prayer: "Dear God, help me be fair and honest like Abraham. Help me treat others right and tell the truth. Help me do what's right even when no one is watching. Amen."

Remember: Being fair and honest builds trust. When people know they can trust you, they want to be your friend!

Chapter 30

Kindness: Being Kind to Others

Being kind means doing nice things for others because you care about them, not because you want something back.

Bible Story: David and Mephibosheth

2 Samuel 9:1-7

King David remembered his best friend, Jonathan, who had died many years before. Jonathan had been so kind to David, even saving his life when Jonathan's own father (King Saul) wanted to hurt David.

One day, David asked, "Is there anyone left from Saul's family that I can show kindness to for Jonathan's sake?"

A servant named Ziba told David, "There is still one of Jonathan's sons living. His name is Mephibosheth. He can't walk well because both his feet are crippled."

"Where is he?" David asked. Ziba told David where to find him.

When Mephibosheth came to the palace, he was afraid! After all, kings often got rid of the previous king's family. He bowed down before David, probably thinking he might be in trouble.

But David said, "Don't be afraid! I want to be kind to you because I loved your father, Jonathan. I will give back all the land that belonged to your grandfather, Saul. And from now on, you will always eat at my table, just like one of my own sons!"

David didn't have to do this, and no one would have blamed him if he ignored Saul's family. But David remembered the kindness Jonathan had shown him, and he wanted to pass that kindness on.

Did You Know? Being kind makes both you AND the other person happy! It's like giving a gift that blesses everyone!

Try This:

Help someone carry something heavy.

Share your snack with someone who doesn't have one.

Say something nice to make someone smile.

Draw a picture for someone who might be feeling sad.

Help a younger child with something they find hard to do.

Prayer: "Dear God, help me be kind like David was. Help me look for ways to help others and make them happy. Thank you for being so kind to me! Amen."

Remember: Jesus said when we are kind to others, it's like we're being kind to Him! Even small acts of kindness make a big difference.

Chapter 31

Loyal: Being Faithful to Others

Being faithful to others means staying with them even when things get hard. It means showing you care by sticking together.

Bible Story: Naomi and Ruth

Ruth 1:1-18

A woman named Naomi lived with her husband and two sons in Bethlehem. When a terrible food shortage (called a famine) happened, they moved to a country called Moab to find food.

While living in Moab, Naomi's husband died. Her two sons married women from Moab named Ruth and Orpah. Then, sadly, both of Naomi's sons died too.

Poor Naomi! She had lost her husband and both sons. She was very sad and decided to go back home to Bethlehem.

She told her daughters-in-law, "Go back to your own mothers' homes. Find new husbands and be happy."

Orpah kissed Naomi goodbye and went back to her family. But Ruth would not leave! She clung to Naomi and said some of the most beautiful words in the Bible:

"Don't ask me to leave you! Where you go, I will go. Where you live, I will live. Your people will be my people, and your God will be my God. Where you die, I will die, and there I will be buried. Only death will separate us!"

Ruth chose to be loyal to Naomi, even though it meant leaving her own country, family, and everything familiar. She stayed with Naomi because she loved her and wanted to take care of her.

God blessed Ruth's loyalty. Later in the story, Ruth meets a kind man named Boaz in Bethlehem, and they get married. Ruth becomes the great-grandmother of King David!

Did You Know? Being loyal to someone means choosing to stick with them, even when it would be easier to leave.

Try This:

Make a loyalty promise to a friend or family member.

Stick up for a friend when others say unkind things.

Keep a promise even when it's hard.

Tell someone, "I'm here for you," when they're having a hard time.

Draw a picture showing how you can be loyal to God.

Prayer: "Dear God, help me be loyal like Ruth was to Naomi. Help me stick with my family and friends even when things get hard. Thank you, Jesus, for never leaving me. Amen."

Remember: Jesus showed the greatest loyalty when He gave His life for us. He said, "Greater love has no one than this: to lay down one's life for one's friends." ~ John 15:13

Chapter 32

Meekness: Being Calm and Patient

Being calm and patient means not getting angry easily. It means waiting your turn and listening to others before you speak.

Bible Story: Elihu and Job

Job32:4-15

In the Bible, a man named Job had many terrible things happen to him. He lost his family, his health, and all his money. Job had three friends who came to talk with him about why these bad things were happening.

A young man named Elihu was also there, listening to everything. Even though Elihu had thoughts and ideas he wanted to share, he waited patiently while the older men spoke first. He showed respect for his elders by being quiet and listening carefully to what everyone had to say.

Elihu said, "I am young, and you are all much older than I am. That's why I was afraid to tell you what I think. I thought to myself, 'Older people should speak first because their many years should have taught them wisdom.'"

Elihu listened to all the conversation between Job and his three friends. Elihu respectfully shared his thoughts only when everyone else had finished speaking.

Even though Elihu disagreed with what the others had said, he stayed calm and spoke kindly. He didn't yell or get angry. He showed that being calm and patient is not being weak - it's actually being very strong!

Did You Know? The Bible says that Moses was the meekest (most humble) man on earth, and yet he was also a great leader who did amazing things with God's help!

Try This:

When you feel angry, take three deep breaths before speaking.

Let others go first in line or in a game.

Listen to what others say without interrupting.

Wait your turn to speak in class or at the dinner table.

Ask God to help you when you feel impatient.

Prayer: "Dear God, help me be calm and patient like Elihu. Help me listen to others and wait my turn. When I feel angry, help me take a deep breath and speak kindly. Amen."

Remember: **Being meek doesn't mean being weak!** It takes great strength to stay calm when others are upset and to be patient when you want something right away.

Chapter 33

Merciful: Showing Kindness When Others Make Mistakes

Showing kindness when others make mistakes means forgiving people when they do wrong things instead of being mean to them. It means giving second chances.

Bible Story: The Unmerciful Servant
Matthew 18:23-35

Jesus told a story about a king who was checking his money books. He found that one of his servants owed him a HUGE amount of money - more than the servant could ever pay back!

The king ordered that the servant and his family be sold as slaves to pay back the debt. The servant fell on his knees and begged, "Please be patient! I'll pay everything back!"

The king felt sorry for the servant and did something amazing - he canceled the entire debt! He told the servant he didn't have to pay back anything at all!

But then, that same servant went out and found another servant who owed him just a tiny bit of money. He grabbed the man by the throat and demanded, "Pay me what you owe!"

The second servant begged, "Please be patient! I'll pay you back!" But the first servant wouldn't listen. He had the man thrown into prison until he could pay.

Other servants saw what happened and told the king. The king was very angry! He called the first servant back, saying, "I canceled your huge debt because you begged me to. Shouldn't you have had mercy on your fellow servant just as I had mercy on you?" Then the king had the unmerciful servant punished.

Jesus told this story to teach us that we should forgive others just as God forgives us.

Did You Know? God has forgiven us for so many mistakes, so we should forgive others, too!

Try This:

When someone makes a mistake, try saying "That's okay" instead of getting angry.

Give someone a second chance when they make a mistake.

Draw a picture of yourself forgiving someone.

Think about a time when someone forgave you and how it made you feel.

Pray for someone who has been unkind to you.

Prayer: "Dear God, help me be merciful like You are. When others make mistakes, help me forgive them instead of being mean. Thank you, Jesus, for forgiving me when I make mistakes. Amen."

Remember: Jesus taught us to pray, "Forgive us our sins, as we forgive those who sin against us." When we are merciful to others, God is merciful to us! ~ Matthew 6:9-13

Chapter 34

Obedience: Listening and Obeying

Listening and obeying means following rules to stay safe and help others, as told to us by parents, teachers, and God.

Bible Story: Jonah Flees From the Lord

Jonah 1:1-17, Jonah 2:1-3, Jonah 2:7-10, and Jonah 3:1-10

God told a man named Jonah, "Go to the city of Nineveh and tell the people there to stop doing bad things, or I will have to punish them."

But Jonah didn't want to go! Instead of obeying God, Jonah ran away. He got on a ship going in the opposite direction, trying to hide from God.

While Jonah was on the ship, a terrible storm came. The waves were so big that the ship was about to break apart!

The sailors were very afraid and began throwing things overboard to make the ship lighter.

Where was Jonah? He was sleeping below deck! The captain woke him up and said, "How can you sleep? Pray to your God to save us!"

The sailors realized someone had done something wrong to cause this storm. They cast lots (like drawing straws), and it showed that Jonah was the problem. Jonah admitted he was running away from God.

"What should we do?" they asked. Jonah said, "Throw me into the sea, and the storm will stop." The sailors didn't want to, but finally they had no choice. As soon as Jonah went into the water, the storm stopped!

But God wasn't finished with Jonah. He sent a huge fish to swallow Jonah! Jonah was inside the fish's belly for three days and three nights. In there, Jonah prayed to God and said he was sorry.

Then God made the fish spit Jonah out onto dry land. God said again, "Go to Nineveh." This time, Jonah obeyed! He went to Nineveh and told the people God's message. The people listened and changed their ways, and God forgave them.

Did You Know? Rules are like guardrails on a mountain road - they keep you from falling over the edge!

Try This:

When a grown-up asks you to do something, do it right away with a smile.

Make a list of rules that keep you safe (like looking both ways before crossing the street).

Practice saying "Yes, I will" when asked to do something.

Thank your parents for the rules that protect you.

Prayer: "Dear God, help me listen and obey like Jonah finally did. Help me follow the rules that keep me safe. Thank you, Jesus, for caring enough to give me rules to follow. Amen."

Remember: Obeying might not always be fun at first, but it keeps us safe and makes life better for everyone!

Chapter 35

Optimistic: Looking on the Bright Side

Looking on the bright side means staying happy even when bad things happen. It means believing that good things will happen.

Bible Story: Paul and Silas in Prison

Acts 16:16-36

Paul and Silas were missionaries who traveled around telling people about Jesus. One day, they met a slave girl who could tell fortunes because she had an evil spirit inside her. Her owners made lots of money from her fortune-telling.

The girl followed Paul and Silas for many days, shouting at them. Finally, Paul felt sorry for her and commanded the evil spirit to leave her in Jesus' name. The girl was healed!

But her owners were very angry because now they couldn't make money from her fortune-telling. They grabbed Paul and Silas and dragged them to the city officials, telling lies about them.

A crowd gathered and attacked Paul and Silas. The officials had them beaten with rods and thrown into the deepest part of the prison with their feet locked in wooden stocks so they couldn't move. This was very painful and uncomfortable!

Now, what would you do if you were beaten up, thrown in jail, and had your feet locked in stocks? Most people would cry or complain. But Paul and Silas did something amazing!

Around midnight, they began praying and singing happy songs to God! The other prisoners were surprised to hear singing coming from the prison. How could anyone be happy in such a terrible situation?

Suddenly, there was a big earthquake that shook the prison! All the doors flew open, and everyone's chains fell off. The jailer woke up and was about to hurt himself because he thought the prisoners had escaped. But Paul shouted, "Don't hurt yourself! We're all still here!"

The jailer was so amazed by their kindness and happiness even in prison that he asked, "What must I do to be saved?" That night, the jailer and his whole family became believers in Jesus.

Did You Know? When you stay positive during hard times, you can help others feel better, too!

Try This:

When something bad happens, try to find one good thing about it.

Sing a happy song when you feel sad.

Make a "Things I'm Thankful For" list.

Say "Today will be a good day!" each morning.

Smile at people who look unhappy - your smile might cheer them up!

Prayer: "Dear God, help me be like Paul and Silas, who sang songs even in jail. Help me stay happy when bad things happen. Thank you, Jesus, for always being with me in good times and hard times. Amen."

Remember: Having a good attitude doesn't change what happens to you, but it does change how you feel about it!

Chapter 36

Patience: Waiting Without Getting Upset

Waiting without getting upset means staying calm even when things aren't going your way. It means not complaining or fighting when you have to wait for something good.

Bible Story: Isaac and the Herdsmen of Gerar
Genesis 26:15-22

There was a man named Isaac who was Abraham's son. Isaac lived in a land where water was very important because it was hot and dry. Without water, people and animals couldn't survive.

Isaac's father, Abraham, had dug many wells to get water. But after Abraham died, the Philistine people filled up all those wells with dirt!

King Abimelech told Isaac, "You must leave our area. You're becoming too powerful for us." So, Isaac moved away to a valley and decided to dig the wells again.

Isaac's workers dug hard and found water in the first well. But the local shepherds came and argued, "This water belongs to us!" Instead of fighting, Isaac simply named the well "Esek," which means "argument," and moved on.

His workers dug a second well. Again, the shepherds claimed it was theirs! Isaac could have been very angry and fought for the well, but instead, he just named it "Sitnah," which means "opposition," and moved on again.

Finally, Isaac's workers dug a third well. This time, no one argued about it! Isaac named this well "Rehoboth," which means "room enough," because he said, "Now the Lord has given us room, and we will be successful in this land."

Isaac finally got what he needed by being patient and not fighting over the wells, and there was peace in the land.

Did You Know? When you stay calm instead of getting angry, you often find better solutions to problems!

Try This:

Count to ten when you feel impatient or angry.

Practice taking deep breaths when you have to wait.

Think of something happy while you're waiting for your turn.

Remember a time when waiting paid off with something good.

Say to yourself, "I can be patient like Isaac".

Prayer: "Dear God, help me be patient like Isaac. When things don't go my way, help me stay calm instead of getting angry. Help me wait without complaining. Thank you for teaching me patience. Amen."

Remember: The Bible says, "Patience is better than pride." ~ Ecclesiastes 7:8-9

Being willing to wait and not fight shows that you're growing up!

Chapter 37

Peaceful: Feeling Calm Inside

Feeling calm inside means trusting God to take care of you, even when scary things happen. It means knowing God is bigger than any problem.

Bible Story: Elisha and the King of Syria

2 Kings 6:8-23

Long ago, the king of Syria was at war with Israel. The king would make secret plans about where to attack, but something strange happened - the king of Israel always knew his plans!

The Syrian king was very upset. "Who is telling our secrets to the enemy?" he asked his helpers.

One of his servants said, "It's not any of us, my king. There's a prophet named Elisha in Israel. God tells him everything - even the words you speak in your bedroom!"

The king decided to capture Elisha. He sent a large army with horses and chariots to the city of Dothan where Elisha was staying. They came at night and surrounded the whole city.

In the morning, Elisha's helper went outside and saw the huge army all around them! He was very afraid and cried, "Oh no, master! What shall we do?"

But Elisha wasn't worried at all. He calmly said, "Don't be afraid. Those who are with us are more than those who are with them."

Then Elisha prayed, "Lord, please open his eyes so he can see." Suddenly, the helper could see something amazing -

the mountain around them was full of horses and chariots of fire! God had sent an army of angels to protect them!

Elisha prayed again, and God made the Syrian soldiers become confused and unable to see clearly. Elisha led them right into the middle of Israel's capital city!

When the king of Israel wanted to kill the captured soldiers, Elisha said, "No! Give them food and water and let them go home." This kindness ended the attacks, and there was peace.

Did You Know? God's peace is special - it gives you calm feelings even when scary things are happening around you!

Try This:

When you feel scared, take three deep breaths and say, "God is with me."

Draw a picture of angels protecting you while you sleep.

Make a "Worry Box" where you can put notes about things that worry you, giving them to God.

Practice being still and quiet for one minute each day.

Remember that God is still in control when you hear about bad news. He will make the crooked paths straight.

Prayer: "Dear God, help me feel peaceful like Elisha, even when scary things happen. Help me remember You're always with me, and You're bigger than any problem. Thank you, Jesus, for protecting me. Amen."

Remember: The Bible says God's peace "passes all understanding." ~ Philippians 4:7

That means God can make you feel calm even when it doesn't make sense to feel calm!

Chapter 38

Perseverance: Keeping On Trying

Perseverance means not giving up when things get hard. It means working through problems and finishing what you start.

Bible Story: Trials and Temptations
James 1:1-27

James was Jesus' brother who wrote a letter to Christians who were having a hard time. In his letter, he shared some important advice about how to keep going when life gets tough.

James wrote, "Consider it pure joy, my brothers and sisters, whenever you face trials of many kinds."

That sounds strange, doesn't it? How can we be happy about problems? James explains that when we go through hard times and keep our faith strong, we develop perseverance - the ability to keep trying even when things are difficult.

James says perseverance helps us grow up spiritually and become complete. It's like exercising a muscle - the more you use it, the stronger it gets! When we face problems and don't give up, our faith becomes stronger.

James also tells us that if we need wisdom to handle our problems, we should ask God. He will give us the wisdom we need if we ask Him with faith, not doubting.

The most wonderful promise James gives is this: "Blessed is the person who perseveres under trial, because when they have stood the test, they will receive the crown of life that God has promised to those who love Him."

This means God has a special reward for people who keep following Him even when it's difficult!

Did You Know? Learning how to walk takes a baby about 1,000 hours of practice! Even after falling down hundreds of times, babies keep trying until they can walk.

Try This:

Make a list of something hard you want to learn (like riding a bike, tying your shoes, or reading).

Break the big goal into smaller steps.

Practice a little bit every day.

When you feel like giving up, remember James' words and keep trying.

Celebrate each small success along the way.

Prayer: "Dear God, help me not give up when things get hard. Help me keep trying like James taught. Thank you, Jesus, for being with me through hard times and helping me grow stronger. Amen."

Remember: "Let us not become weary in doing good, for at the proper time we will reap a harvest if we do not give up!" ~ Galatians 6:9

Chapter 39

Persuasive: Explaining Things Well to Others

Persuasive means helping people understand God's truth in a kind, clear way. It means knowing how to share what you believe.

Bible Story: Philip and the Ethiopian
Acts 8:26-40

One day, an angel appeared to a man named Philip and told him, "Get up and go south on the desert road from Jerusalem to Gaza."

Philip obeyed right away. As he was walking along the road, he saw a chariot. Inside was an important man from Ethiopia who worked for the Ethiopian queen. This man had traveled all the way to Jerusalem to worship God and was now returning home.

The Holy Spirit told Philip, "Go over to that chariot and stay near it."

Philip ran up to the chariot and heard the man reading aloud from the book of Isaiah in the Bible. Philip asked him, "Do you understand what you're reading?"

The man replied honestly, "How can I understand unless someone explains it to me?" Then he invited Philip to climb into the chariot and sit with him.

The Ethiopian was reading a part of the Bible that talked about someone who would suffer like a lamb led to slaughter. He asked Philip, "Who is this talking about? Is the prophet talking about himself or someone else?"

This was Philip's chance! He began with that same Scripture and explained how it was talking about Jesus. He told the Ethiopian all about Jesus' life, death, and resurrection.

The Ethiopian believed what Philip told him. When they passed some water, he asked, "Look! Here's water! What would stop me from being baptized right now?"

Philip baptized him right there. When they came up out of the water, Philip suddenly disappeared! The Holy Spirit had taken him away. The Ethiopian went on his way, happy because he now understood God's truth.

Did You Know? Being persuasive doesn't mean being pushy or loud. The best way to help someone understand is to be kind, patient, and honest!

Try This:

Practice explaining something you know well (like a game or hobby) to someone else.

When someone asks a question you can't answer, say "I don't know, but I can try to find out."

Listen carefully to what others say before you answer.

Think about how to explain things in ways that make sense to different people.

Remember that showing kindness is just as important as having the right answers.

Prayer: "Dear God, help me explain Your truth to others like Philip did. Help me be kind and clear when I talk about you. Thank you for people who have helped me understand Your Word. Amen."

Remember: "Always be prepared to give an answer to everyone who asks you to give the reason for the hope that you have. But do this with gentleness and respect." ~1 Peter 3:15

Chapter 40

Prompt: Being Ready and On Time

Being Prompt means not making people wait for you. It means doing what you're asked to do right away, not later.

Bible Story: The Parable of the Ten Virgins

Matthew 25:1-13

Jesus told a story about ten young women who were waiting for a wedding to begin. In those days, weddings often happened at night, so everyone carried oil lamps to light their way.

Five of these young women were wise and prepared. They brought extra oil for their lamps in case they had to wait a long time. The other five were foolish and only had the oil that was already in their lamps.

They all waited for the bridegroom (like the groom at a wedding) to arrive. He was taking so long that they all fell asleep!

At midnight, someone shouted, "The bridegroom is coming! Come out to meet him!"

All ten women woke up and checked their lamps. The wise ones' lamps were still burning brightly. But the foolish ones' lamps were going out because they had used up all their oil.

The foolish women asked the wise ones, "Please give us some of your oil!"

The wise ones replied, "We can't - there won't be enough for all of us. You should go to the store and buy more oil."

While the foolish women were gone buying oil, the bridegroom arrived! The five wise women, who were ready, went with him into the wedding feast. Then the door was closed and locked.

Later, the other five women came back with their oil. They knocked on the door calling, "Sir! Sir! Let us in!"

But he answered, "I don't know you." And they missed the whole celebration!

Jesus told this story to teach us to always be ready and prepared.

Did You Know? Being late for important events has been a problem for people throughout history! That's why there are so many sayings like "The early bird gets the worm."

Try This:

Set your clothes out the night before school so you're not rushing in the morning.

When your parents ask you to do something, do it right away.

Make a chart of things you need to do each day, so you don't forget.

Set an alarm 5 minutes earlier than you think you need to wake up.

Practice saying "I'll do it now" instead of "I'll do it later."

Prayer: "Dear God, help me be ready and on time like the five wise women. Help me not put off until tomorrow what I should do today. Thank You for teaching me to be responsible. Amen."

Remember: When prompt and ready, show others that you respect their time and that they can count on you!

Chapter 41

Prudent: Planning Carefully

Prudent means thinking before you act. It means making a good plan and following it step by step.

Bible Story: Esther Saves Her People from Haman

Esther 3:8-9, Esther 4:1-3, 6-8, Esther 5:1-4, Esther 7:1-10

Long ago, a beautiful Jewish woman named Esther became queen of Persia. The king didn't know she was Jewish.

A wicked man named Haman worked for the king. Haman hated the Jewish people, especially Esther's cousin Mordecai, who wouldn't bow down to him. Haman was so angry that he tricked the king into making a law that would kill all the Jewish people in the kingdom!

When Mordecai heard about this terrible plan, he sent a message to Queen Esther: "You must go to the king and beg him to save our people!"

This put Esther in a very difficult situation. In those days, no one could approach the king without being invited - not even the queen! Anyone who did might be put to death, unless the king held out his golden scepter to them.

Esther needed a careful plan. She couldn't just rush in and demand that the king change the law. Instead, she made a smart plan:

First, she asked all the Jewish people to pray and fast (not eat) for three days.

Then, she put on her most beautiful royal robes and carefully approached the king. When the king saw her, he was pleased and held out his golden scepter.

Instead of telling him everything right away, Esther invited the king and Haman to a special dinner. At the dinner, she didn't make her request yet - she invited them to a second dinner the next day!

At the second dinner, Esther finally revealed her request: "Please spare my life and the lives of my people." She told the king that Haman was planning to kill all the Jews, including her!

The king was furious with Haman. Haman was punished, and Esther's careful planning saved the Jewish people.

Did You Know? The expression "look before you leap" means to think carefully before you take action, just like Esther did!

Try This:

Before starting a big project, make a list of all the steps you'll need to take.

Ask someone with experience for advice when you're not sure what to do.

Think about what might go wrong with your plan and how you could fix it.

Practice being patient even when you want to rush.

Draw a picture of Esther's careful plan and how it worked.

Prayer: "Dear God, help me be careful and wise like Queen Esther. Help me think before I act and make good plans. Thank you for the people who give me good advice. Amen."

Remember: "The plans of the diligent lead to profit, but hasty plans lead to poverty." ~ Proverbs 21:5

Chapter 42

Purposeful: Doing Your Best for God

Doing your best for God means finding out what special job God wants you to do and doing it with all your heart.

Bible Story: The Calling of Moses

Exodus 3:1-14

Moses was taking care of his father-in-law's sheep in the desert. One day, he saw something very strange - a bush that was on fire but wasn't burning up!

Moses said, "I need to go see this amazing sight!"

As Moses got closer, God called to him from the burning bush, "Moses! Moses!"

Moses answered, "Here I am."

God told him, "Don't come any closer. Take off your sandals, because you're standing on holy ground. I am the

God of your ancestors - Abraham, Isaac, and Jacob." Moses hid his face because he was afraid to look at God.

Then God told Moses something important: "I have seen how my people are suffering in Egypt. I have heard their cries. I am going to rescue them and bring them to a good land. And Moses, I am sending YOU to lead them out!"

Moses was surprised! "Me? Who am I to do such a big job? Why should I go to Pharaoh? Why should I lead the Israelites?"

God answered, "I will be with you! When you bring the people out of Egypt, you will worship me on this mountain. That will be the sign that I sent you."

Moses was still worried. "What if they ask me who sent me? What should I tell them?"

God said, "Tell them 'I AM' has sent you. That is my name forever."

Moses was afraid at first, but he finally agreed to do what God asked. He became one of the greatest leaders in the Bible because he found his purpose and followed God's plan.

Did You Know? Just like Moses, God has a special job for you, too! It might not be leading a whole nation, but God has something important for you to do.

Try This:

Ask God to show you what special talents He gave you.

Do your schoolwork and chores with your whole heart, as if you're doing them for God.

Look for ways to help others using your special abilities.

Make a list of things you're good at and think about how you could use them to serve God.

Draw a picture of yourself doing something special for God.

Prayer: "Dear God, help me know what special job You have for me. Help me do my best at everything, not halfway. Thank you for having a purpose for my life. Amen."

Remember: "Whatever you do, work at it with all your heart, as working for the Lord." ~ Colossians 3:23

Chapter 43

Resourceful: Finding Creative Ways to Help

Finding creative ways to help means using your imagination to solve problems and do more than what's expected. It means being willing to go the extra mile.

Bible Story: Isaac and Rebekah

Genesis 24:1-51

Abraham was very old and wanted to find a wife for his son, Isaac. Since they lived far from their relatives, Abraham sent his trusted servant on a special mission to find the right woman.

The servant traveled a long way with ten camels loaded with gifts. When he arrived at a town, he stopped by a well where women came to get water. He prayed to God, "Please help me find the right wife for Isaac. Let it be the woman who not only gives me a drink when I ask, but also offers to water my camels."

This was asking for someone very special! Watering ten thirsty camels would be a HUGE job. One camel can drink up to 30 gallons of water! The person would need to make many trips back and forth to the well with a heavy water jar.

Just then, a beautiful young woman named Rebekah came to the well. The servant asked her for a drink, and she quickly gave him water. Then, without being asked, Rebekah said, "I'll also draw water for all your camels!"

Rebekah worked hard, going back and forth to the well many times until all ten camels had enough to drink. She didn't have to do this extra work, but she was a kind and resourceful person.

The servant knew this must be the woman God had chosen for Isaac! He gave Rebekah gold jewelry and asked about her family. When he met her family and explained his mission, they agreed that Rebekah should marry Isaac.

Because Rebekah was willing to do more than expected, she became Isaac's wife and part of God's special plan!

Did You Know? A camel can drink up to 30 gallons of water in just 13 minutes! That means Rebekah probably carried hundreds of pounds of water to help those ten camels.

Try This:

Look for ways to help without being asked.

Think of a chore you do regularly and find a better way to do it.

Fix something broken instead of throwing it away.

Use old items in new ways (like making a pencil holder from an empty can).

Help someone with a job that seems too big for them.

Prayer: "Dear God, help me be resourceful like Rebekah. Help me find creative ways to solve problems and help others. Thank you for the special abilities you've given me. Amen."

Remember: Being resourceful isn't about having everything you need - it's about making the most of what you have!

Chapter 44

Respectful: Honoring Those in Charge

Honoring those in charge means showing respect to parents, teachers, and leaders. It means treating them with kindness and obeying their good instructions.

Bible Story: David Spares Saul's Life

1 Samuel 24:1-22

King Saul tried to kill David because he was jealous of him. David had to hide in the wilderness to stay safe. One day, Saul came into a cave where David and his men were hiding far in the back. Saul didn't see them because it was dark.

David's friends whispered excitedly, "This is your chance! God has given your enemy to you. You can kill him now!" David quietly crept forward and cut off a small piece of Saul's robe, but he wouldn't hurt Saul.

Afterward, David felt bad even for cutting Saul's robe. He told his men, "I will not hurt the king. He is the Lord's chosen one." David stopped his men from attacking Saul.

After Saul left the cave, David came out and called, "My lord the king!" Saul turned around, and David bowed down with his face to the ground to show respect.

David said, "Look, today God put you in my power in the cave. Some told me to kill you, but I spared you. See this piece of your robe in my hand? I cut it off, but I didn't hurt you. I have done nothing wrong to you, yet you're trying to kill me."

When Saul heard this, he cried and said, "You are more righteous than I am! You have treated me well, even though I've treated you badly. When a man finds his enemy, does he let him go unhurt? May God reward you for what you've done today."

Because David respected Saul's position as king, even when Saul was wrong, God later made David the new king of Israel.

Did You Know? In many cultures around the world, children stand up when adults enter the room to show respect!

Try This:

Say "please" and "thank you" to your parents and teachers.

Listen quietly when adults are talking instead of interrupting.

Obey rules at home and school without complaining.

Stand up straight and look at people when they talk to you.

Help your parents or teachers without being asked.

Prayer: "Dear God, help me be respectful like David was. Help me honor my parents, teachers, and leaders even when it's hard. Thank you for putting special people in my life to guide me. Amen."

Remember: "Honor your father and your mother, so that you may live long in the land the Lord your God is giving you." ~ Exodus 20:12

Chapter 45

Responsible: Doing What You're Supposed to Do

Doing what you're supposed to do means taking care of your jobs and responsibilities without being reminded. It means being someone others can count on.

Bible Story: Aaron and His Sons Bear the Responsibility of Setting Up the Tabernacle

Numbers 4:1-15

Long ago, God gave Moses plans for a special tent called the Tabernacle where people would worship. It was like a portable church that could be moved when the Israelites traveled.

God chose Aaron (Moses' brother) and his sons to be the priests who would take care of the Tabernacle. Each person in Aaron's family had special jobs they needed to do. God gave very clear instructions about these jobs.

When it was time to move the camp, Aaron and his sons had to carefully pack up all the holy things in the Tabernacle:

They covered the special Ark with a beautiful veil and leather

They wrapped the table of holy bread in blue cloth

They covered the golden lampstand and all its parts

They wrapped all the special tools used for worship

Only after Aaron and his sons finished their job could the other workers (the Kohathites) come to carry these holy items. If anyone tried to touch the holy things before they were properly wrapped, or if they didn't follow instructions exactly, they could die! That's how important these responsibilities were.

Each person had to do their part exactly right. If even one person didn't do their job, the whole system wouldn't work, and God wouldn't be properly worshipped.

Did You Know? God gave each of us different responsibilities based on our abilities. When everyone does their part, amazing things can happen!

Try This:

Make a list of your responsibilities at home and school.

Finish your chores without being reminded.

When you see something that needs to be done, do it without being asked.

After using something, put it away where it belongs.

Take care of your pets, toys, or belongings without someone telling you to.

Prayer: "Dear God, help me be responsible like Aaron and his sons. Help me do my chores well and on time. Help me remember that my responsibilities are important, even when they seem small. Amen."

Remember: "Whoever can be trusted with very little can also be trusted with much." ~ Luke 16:10

You'll be given bigger responsibilities when you show you're responsible for small things!

Chapter 46

Secure: Feeling Safe with God

Feeling safe with God means knowing God is protecting you, so you don't have to be afraid. It means trusting God to take care of you.

Bible Story: Daniel in the Lion's Den
Daniel 6:1-28

King Darius put Daniel in charge of many important leaders in his kingdom. Daniel did such a good job that the king planned to put him in charge of everything!

This made the other leaders jealous. They looked for ways to get Daniel in trouble, but they couldn't find anything wrong with his work. Daniel was honest and did everything right.

Finally, these jealous men had an idea. They knew Daniel prayed to God every day. So they tricked the king into making a new law: "For thirty days, no one can pray to any god or person except to King Darius. Anyone who breaks this law will be thrown into a den of lions!"

When Daniel heard about this new law, what do you think he did? Did he stop praying? No! Daniel went home, opened his windows toward Jerusalem, and prayed to God three times a day, just like he always did.

The jealous men saw Daniel praying and told the king. King Darius was very upset because he liked Daniel, but he couldn't change the law. So, Daniel was thrown into a den of hungry lions!

Before they closed the den, the king said to Daniel, "May your God, whom you serve faithfully, rescue you!"

The king couldn't sleep all night because he was worried about Daniel. Early the next morning, he hurried to the lions' den and called out, "Daniel, has your God been able to save you from the lions?"

Daniel answered, "My God sent His angel to shut the lions' mouths! They haven't hurt me at all because I was innocent in God's sight."

The king was overjoyed! He had Daniel lifted out of the den, and there wasn't a scratch on him. Daniel was safe because he trusted in God.

Did You Know? God promises to be with us always, even in scary situations. That doesn't mean nothing bad will ever happen, but it means God is always with us no matter what.

Try This:

When you feel afraid, say this prayer: "God, thank You for protecting me."

Draw a picture of Daniel in the lions' den with an angel shutting the lions' mouths.

Make a list of times when God kept you safe.

When you're scared at night, remember that God never sleeps and is watching over you.

Share the story of Daniel with a friend who is feeling afraid.

Prayer: "Dear God, help me be brave like Daniel. When I feel afraid, help me remember that You are with me and protecting me. Thank you for keeping me safe. Amen."

Remember: "God has not given us a spirit of fear, but of power and of love and of a sound mind." ~ 2 Timothy 1:7

Chapter 47

Self-Control: Being in Control of Yourself

Being in control of yourself means choosing how you react when people make you mad. It means not hitting, shouting, or saying mean things when you feel angry.

Bible Story: David Shows Restraint
2 Samuel 16:5-14

King David was having a very hard time. His own son, Absalom, was trying to take over his kingdom! David had to leave Jerusalem and run away with his loyal followers.

As David and his men were walking along a road, a man named Shimei came out and started causing trouble. Shimei was from the family of the previous king, Saul, and he was very angry at David.

Shimei did three terrible things:

He shouted mean words and called David awful names

He threw rocks at David and his soldiers

He threw dust in the air to show how much he hated David

One of David's soldiers, Abishai, got very angry. He said to David, "Why are you letting this man talk to you like that? Let me go cut off his head!"

But David showed amazing self-control. Instead of getting angry or letting his soldier hurt Shimei, David said, "No, leave him alone. Maybe God has told him to say these things. Maybe God will see how I'm suffering and turn this bad situation into something good."

So, David and his men just kept walking, even though Shimei kept following them, throwing rocks and shouting mean things.

David chose to control his feelings instead of fighting back. Later, God helped David return to his kingdom safely.

Did You Know? Your brain has a special part called the "prefrontal cortex" that helps you control your actions when you feel angry. This part of your brain keeps growing until you're about 25 years old!

Try This:

When you feel angry, count to ten before saying anything.

Take three deep breaths when someone upsets you.

Walk away from a situation that makes you want to yell or hit.

Use your words to tell someone how you feel instead of acting out.

Practice saying, "I need a moment to calm down" when you're upset.

Prayer: "Dear God, help me control myself like David did. When people make me angry, help me choose kind words and peaceful actions. Thank you for giving me the power to control how I act. Amen."

Remember: "A person without self-control is like a city with broken-down walls." ~ Proverbs 25:28

Self-control protects you and keeps you safe!

Chapter 48

Sincere: Being Honest and True

Being honest and true means having pure motives and not trying to trick people. It means doing the right thing because it's right, not because you'll get something out of it.

Bible Story: The Story of Abimelech
Judges 9:1-24

There was once a man named Gideon (also called Jerubbaal) with seventy sons. One of his sons, Abimelech, was born to Gideon's servant woman.

Abimelech wanted to be king but knew his brothers would be chosen first. So, he went to his mother's relatives in Shechem and said, "Ask everyone in town: 'Which would be better - to have all seventy of Gideon's sons rule over you, or just one man?' Remember, I'm your relative!"

Abimelech wasn't being honest. He didn't really care what was best for the people - he just wanted power for himself.

The people of Shechem gave Abimelech money, which he used to hire some troublemakers to help him. Then Abimelech did something terrible - he killed all of his brothers except for Jotham, the youngest, who escaped by hiding.

The people of Shechem made Abimelech their king, not knowing how evil he truly was.

When Jotham heard what happened, he climbed a mountain and shouted to the people. He told them a story about trees looking for a king. The olive tree, fig tree, and grapevine all refused to be king because they were busy doing good things. Finally, the thornbush (which produces nothing good) became king.

Jotham's story was a warning: Abimelech was like the thornbush - he couldn't offer anything good, only harm.

After three years, God caused trouble between Abimelech and the people of Shechem. They turned against each other, and in the fighting, both Abimelech and the people who helped him were destroyed.

Abimelech wasn't sincere or honest, and his dishonesty led to his downfall.

Did You Know? The word "sincere" comes from Latin words that mean "without wax." Long ago, dishonest pottery sellers would fill cracks with wax to hide them. Truly good pottery was "without wax" - sincere!

Try This:

Tell the truth even when no one would know if you didn't.

Keep your promises, even small ones.

Don't pretend to like something just because your friends do.

When you do something nice, do it because it's right, not to get a reward.

If you make a mistake, admit it instead of blaming someone else.

Prayer: "Dear God, help me be honest and true like You want me to be. Help me have pure motives for the things I do. Thank you for seeing my heart and helping me grow. Amen."

Remember: "The Lord detests lying lips, but He delights in people who are trustworthy." ~ Proverbs 12:22

Chapter 49

Submissive: Following Good Leaders

Following good leaders means listening to parents, teachers, and others who help you make good choices. It means being willing to let others lead when it's right.

Bible Story: Jesus Prays on the Mount of Olives
Luke 22:39-44

The night before Jesus was going to die on the cross, He went to a garden called the Mount of Olives to pray. His disciples came with Him.

When they arrived, Jesus told His disciples, "Pray that you won't fall into temptation." Then Jesus went a little farther away by Himself to pray alone.

Jesus knelt down and prayed one of the most important prayers ever: "Father, if You are willing, take this cup from me. Yet not my will, but Yours be done."

Jesus knew something very hard was about to happen. He was going to suffer and die on the cross for everyone's sins. As a human, Jesus didn't want to go through such terrible pain. That's what He meant by asking God to "take this cup" away.

But Jesus showed us what it means to be submissive to God. Even though He didn't want to suffer, He said, "Not my will, but Yours be done." Jesus was willing to follow God's plan instead of His own wishes.

Jesus was in such deep prayer that He began to sweat drops like blood! An angel came from heaven to give Him strength.

Jesus wasn't weak when He submitted to God's plan. It actually took incredible strength to say, "I'll do it Your way, not mine." Because Jesus was willing to follow God's plan, He saved the whole world!

Did You Know? Being submissive doesn't mean being weak! Sometimes, it takes great strength to let someone else lead. The strongest leaders know when to follow.

Try This:

Practice saying "Yes, I will" when your parents ask you to do something.

When playing games, take turns being the leader and the follower.

Think about rules at home or school - how do they help keep you safe?

When you're asked to do something, ask yourself, "Would this make God happy?"

Draw a picture of Jesus praying in the garden.

Prayer: "Dear God, help me be like Jesus who followed Your plan even when it was hard. Help me listen to my parents, teachers, and other good leaders. Help me know when I should say 'not my way, but Yours.' Amen."

Remember: "Submit to one another out of reverence for Christ." ~ Ephesians 5:21

When we follow good leaders, we're showing love for God!

Chapter 50

Supportive: Helping Others Succeed

Helping others succeed means encouraging people and giving them the support they need. It means being there for others when they need help.

Bible Story: The Amalekites Defeated

Exodus 17:8-13

The Israelites were traveling through the wilderness when a group called the Amalekites attacked them.

Moses told Joshua, "Choose some men and go fight against the Amalekites. Tomorrow I will stand on top of the hill holding God's special staff in my hands."

The next day, Joshua led the soldiers into battle while Moses, Aaron, and Hur went up on a hill where they could see everything. Moses held up the staff of God in his hands.

Something amazing happened! Whenever Moses held his hands up high, the Israelites started winning the battle. But whenever Moses got tired and lowered his hands, the Amalekites started winning instead!

Moses' arms got very tired - he couldn't keep them up all day by himself. So, Aaron and Hur had a good idea. First, they found a large stone for Moses to sit on so he could rest. Then, they stood on either side of Moses and held up his hands - Aaron on one side and Hur on the other.

They kept Moses' hands steady and lifted them high until the sun went down. Because of their help and support, Joshua and the Israelite army were able to win the battle against the Amalekites!

This story shows us that everyone needs help sometimes. Even Moses, the great leader, couldn't win the battle alone.

It took Joshua fighting, Moses praying, and Aaron and Hur supporting Moses' arms to win the victory.

Did You Know? Scientists have found that people who have supportive friends and family are usually healthier and happier than people who try to do everything alone!

Try This:

Say something encouraging to a friend or family member today.

Help someone with a hard job they can't do alone.

Draw a picture of yourself helping someone who needs support.

Cheer for your classmates or siblings when they're doing something difficult.

Ask someone who seems sad if there's anything you can do to help them.

Prayer: "Dear God, help me be like Aaron and Hur, who supported Moses' arms. Show me how I can help and encourage others today. Thank you for the people who support me. Amen."

Remember: "Two people are better than one. They can help each other in everything they do. If one person falls, the other can reach out and help." ~ Ecclesiastes 4:9-10

Chapter 51

Tactful: Using Kind Words When Helping Others

Using kind words when helping others means giving advice in a gentle way. It means finding the right words that show you care about someone's feelings.

Bible Story: Jethro Visits Moses

Exodus 18:7-27

Moses had led the Israelites out of Egypt and was now their leader in the wilderness. Moses' father-in-law, Jethro, came to visit him.

When Jethro arrived, Moses greeted him warmly. They went into Moses' tent, and Moses told Jethro all about their amazing journey - how God had rescued them from Egypt and protected them along the way.

Jethro was so happy to hear about God's goodness! He said, "Praise be to the Lord who rescued you from the Egyptians! Now I know that the Lord is greater than all other gods!"

The next day, Jethro watched Moses at work. From morning until night, Moses sat as a judge while all the people stood around waiting to ask him questions or settle their arguments.

Jethro noticed that Moses looked very tired. Both Moses and the people were wearing themselves out with this system. Jethro could have said, "Moses, you're being foolish! Can't you see this isn't working?" But instead, he was tactful and kind.

First, Jethro asked Moses a question: "What are you doing for the people? Why do you alone sit as judge while everyone stands around waiting?"

After Moses explained, Jethro gently said, "What you're doing is not good. You and the people will wear yourselves out. The work is too heavy for you to handle alone."

Then, instead of just pointing out the problem, Jethro offered a helpful solution: "Choose trustworthy men to be judges over groups of people. Let them handle the simple cases, and only bring the difficult ones to you."

Moses wasn't upset by Jethro's advice because it was given with kindness and respect. Moses listened and followed Jethro's suggestion, which made life better for everyone!

Did You Know? Studies show that people are much more likely to accept advice when given in a kind, respectful way rather than when someone tells them they're wrong!

Try This:

Before giving advice, think about how your words might make the other person feel.

Use "sandwich feedback" - say something nice, then give advice, then say something nice again.

Ask questions instead of telling someone what to do (like Jethro did with Moses).

Practice saying "Have you thought about..." instead of "You should...".

Role-play with a friend or parent to practice giving advice in a kind way.

Prayer: "Dear God, help me use kind words when I need to help others. Give me wisdom to know what to say and how to say it. Help me be tactful like Jethro. Amen."

Remember: "Gracious words are like honeycomb, sweet to the soul and healing to the bones." ~ Proverbs 16:24

Chapter 52

Temperate: Wanting Just Enough

Wanting just enough means being happy with what you need instead of always wanting more. It means controlling your wants, so you don't make bad choices.

Bible Story: Abram and Lot Part Ways
Genesis 13:1-18

Abram (later called Abraham) and his nephew Lot had traveled together for a long time. Both of them had many animals and servants. They had so many sheep, goats, and cattle that the land couldn't support all their animals in one place!

Their shepherds started arguing over grass and water for the animals. When Abram heard about these arguments, he went to Lot and said, "Let's not have any quarreling between us or between our shepherds. We are family! There's plenty of land - let's separate. If you go to the left, I'll go to the right. If you go to the right, I'll go to the left."

Abram, even though he was older and could have chosen first, let Lot choose which land he wanted. This showed that Abram was not greedy.

Lot looked around and saw the Jordan Valley. It was green and well-watered, "like the garden of the Lord." Lot chose all the Jordan Valley for himself and moved his tents near Sodom.

But there was a big problem with Lot's choice. The Bible says, "The men of Sodom were wicked and were sinning greatly against the Lord." Lot only looked at how good the land was - he didn't think about his neighbors.

Abram settled in Canaan, away from the wicked cities. After Lot left, God spoke to Abram and promised to give him and his descendants all the land he could see in every direction. God blessed Abram because he wasn't greedy.

Later in the Bible, we learn that Lot lost everything when God destroyed the wicked city of Sodom. His greedy choice led to trouble!

Did You Know? Studies show that people who focus on having lots of things are often less happy than people who focus on experiences and relationships!

Try This:

Make a list of things you're thankful for that you already have.

Choose one toy or game you don't play with anymore and give it to someone who would enjoy it.

When you want something new, wait a week before asking for it to see if you still want it.

Practice saying "What I have is enough" when you see something new you want.

Think about the character of friends you choose, not just the fun things they might have.

Prayer: "Dear God, help me be happy with what I have, like Abram was. Help me make good choices that won't lead to trouble. Thank you for giving me everything I need. Amen."

Remember: "Keep your lives free from the love of money and be content with what you have, because God has said, 'Never will I leave you; never will I forsake you.'" ~ Hebrews 13:5

Chapter 53

Thankful: Saying Thank You

Saying thank you means showing gratitude when people are kind to you. It means telling God and others how much you appreciate what they've done for you.

Bible Story: The Story of Hannah

1 Samuel 1:1-20 and 1 Samuel 2:1

A woman named Hannah was very sad because she had no children. Her husband, Elkanah, had another wife named Peninnah who had several children, and Peninnah often teased Hannah about not having any kids.

Every year, Hannah's family would travel to worship God at a place called Shiloh. One year, Hannah was feeling especially sad. After they finished eating, Hannah went to the temple to pray.

With tears streaming down her face, Hannah prayed, "Lord, if You will give me a son, I promise I will give him back to You. He will serve you all his life."

As Hannah prayed silently, only her lips were moving. Eli, the priest, saw her and thought she was drunk! He scolded her, "How long will you keep on being drunk? Put away your wine!"

Hannah respectfully explained, "I'm not drunk, sir. I'm just very sad, and I've been pouring out my heart to the Lord."

Eli then blessed her and said, "May God give you what you've asked for."

Hannah felt much better after praying. She went back to her family, ate some food, and wasn't sad anymore.

God heard Hannah's prayer! Before long, she had a baby boy and named him Samuel, which means "heard by God." Hannah was so thankful to God for answering her prayer!

When Samuel was old enough, Hannah kept her promise. She took him to the temple and gave him to Eli so Samuel could serve God his whole life. Even though it must have been hard to give up her son, Hannah was still thankful. She sang a beautiful prayer of thanks to God.

Samuel grew up to become one of Israel's greatest prophets, all because his mother was thankful and kept her promise to God.

Did You Know? People who regularly express thankfulness are often happier and healthier than people who complain a lot!

Try This:

Make a "Thank You" card for someone who has helped you.

Start a thankfulness journal - write down three things you're thankful for each day.

Say "thank you" to your parents or caregivers for making your meals.

Tell God "thank you" in your prayers for specific blessings.

Make a "Gratitude Chain" - write something you're thankful for on a strip of paper each day and link them together.

Prayer: "Dear God, thank You for all the good things in my life. Help me remember to say 'thank you' to you and to others who help me. Like Hannah, help me keep my promises and show my gratitude. Amen."

Remember: "Give thanks in all circumstances, for this is God's will for you." ~ 1 Thessalonians 5:18

Chapter 54

Thorough: Completing Every Task

Thorough means doing ALL of a job. It means not missing any parts. It means doing your best work!

Bible Story: Joshua Defeats The Northern Kings

Joshua 11:6-15

God told Joshua, "Do not be afraid. I will help you win the battle."

Joshua listened carefully to ALL of God's plan. He needed to:

Fight the enemy kings.

Make sure their horses couldn't run.

Burn their chariots.

Joshua did EVERYTHING God told him to do. He didn't skip any steps. He was thorough!

The Bible says: "Joshua did it; he left nothing undone of all that the LORD commanded."

Did You Know? Bees are very thorough! When a bee visits a flower, it checks EVERY part where nectar might be hiding. This helps the bee get all the sweet nectar and helps the flower make seeds.

Try This:

Make a checklist for something you do every day, like getting ready for school. Check off each step as you finish it. See if being thorough helps you do a better job!

Items for your checklist:

Brush teeth

Pack lunch

Put homework in the backpack

Tie shoes

Prayer: "Dear God, help me to be thorough like Joshua. Help me remember all the parts of what I need to do. Thank you for showing me how to do my best. Amen."

Remember: "Whatever you do, work at it with all your heart, as working for the Lord." ~ Colossians 3:23

Chapter 55

Thoughtful: Caring About Others

Thoughtful means caring about other people's feelings, being kind and helpful to others, and thinking about what others need!

Bible Story: The Story of Rahab

Joshua 2:1-21

Joshua sent two men to look at the city of Jericho. They stayed at Rahab's house.

The king wanted to catch these men. But Rahab was thoughtful. She hid the men on her roof under some flax plants.

Rahab told the king's men, "They left already. Go catch them!" This wasn't true, but she wanted to protect the visitors.

Later, Rahab helped the men escape through her window with a rope. She asked them to save her family when they came back.

The men said, "We will be kind to you because you were kind to us! Hang a red rope from your window so we know which house is yours."

Did You Know? Elephants are very thoughtful animals! When a baby elephant is scared or sad, other elephants will touch it gently with their trunks to make it feel better. They even remember friends they haven't seen for many years!

Try This:

Make a "Thoughtful Jar." When you see someone do something nice, write it on a small piece of paper and put it in the jar. At the end of the week, read all the thoughtful things people did!

Some thoughtful things you could do:

Share your snack

Help clean up

Let someone go first

Say "thank you."

Prayer: "Dear God, help me be thoughtful like Rahab. Help me see when others need help or kindness. Thank you for teaching me how to care about others. Amen."

Remember: "Look not only to your own interests, but also to the interests of others." ~ Philippians 2:4

Chapter 56

Thrifty: Using Money Wisely

Thrifty means using money and things carefully. It means not wasting what you have. It's making smart choices with what God gives you!

Bible Story: Jacob's Wages

Genesis 30:25-43

Jacob worked for Laban for many years. He took care of Laban's sheep and goats.

One day, Jacob said, "I want to go home with my family. I have worked hard for you."

Laban didn't want Jacob to leave. He asked, "What can I pay you to stay?"

Jacob had a smart plan. He said, "Let me have the spotted and speckled animals from your flocks."

Laban agreed. Then Jacob used clever ways to help more spotted and speckled animals be born. He put special sticks near the water where the animals drank.

Over time, Jacob's flock grew bigger and bigger. Jacob became rich with many animals by being smart with what he had.

Did You Know? Squirrels are very thrifty animals! They collect nuts and seeds all summer and fall. Then they hide them in many places to eat during winter when food is hard to find. A single squirrel can hide thousands of nuts!

Try This:

Make a savings jar for your coins. Decorate it with pictures of something you want to buy. Each time you get money, put some in your jar. Count how long it takes to save enough!

Ways to be thrifty:

Turn off the lights when you leave a room.

Use both sides of the paper for drawing.

Take good care of your toys so they last longer.

Share books with friends instead of buying new ones.

Prayer: "Dear God, help me be thrifty like Jacob. Help me use my things carefully and not waste what you give me. Thank you for teaching me to be wise with what I have. Amen."

Remember: "The wise store up choice food and olive oil, but fools gulp theirs down." ~ Proverbs 21:20

Chapter 57

Tolerant: Showing Respect

Being Tolerant means showing respect for people who are different from you. It also means being patient with others and accepting them, even when they have different ideas or ways of doing things.

Bible Story: Paul and Cornelius
Acts 10:9-44

Peter was praying on a rooftop when he had a strange vision. God showed him a big sheet coming down from heaven. It was filled with many animals that Jews were not allowed to eat.

God told Peter, "Rise up, Peter, kill and eat."

Peter said, "No, Lord! I've never eaten anything unclean."

God answered, "Do not call unclean what I have made clean." This happened three times!

Soon after, men came looking for Peter. They were sent by a Roman officer named Cornelius. Romans and Jews didn't usually spend time together.

The Holy Spirit told Peter, "Go with these men. Don't hesitate."

Peter went to Cornelius's house, even though Jews weren't supposed to visit non-Jewish homes. Peter told everyone, "God has shown me that I should not call any person unclean or common."

Peter learned that God loves all people, no matter where they come from. He shared Jesus' story with Cornelius and his family, and the Holy Spirit came to them too!

Did You Know? In Japan, people take off their shoes before entering a house. In America, many people keep their shoes on inside. Different cultures have different ways of showing respect, and being tolerant means learning about these differences!

Try This:

Make a "Different Is Good" poster. Draw pictures of children from around the world. Write down things you can learn from people who are different from you.

Ways to be tolerant:

Listen when someone has a different idea.

Try foods from other countries.

Learn how to say "hello" in different languages.

Ask questions instead of making fun of differences.

Prayer: "Dear God, help me be tolerant like Peter. Help me respect people who are different from me. Thank you for making all kinds of people and teaching us to love everyone. Amen."

Remember: "Accept one another, just as Christ accepted you." ~ Romans 15:7

Chapter 58

Truthful: Speaking What is True

Truthful means saying what is real and right. It means not telling lies, even small ones. It means being honest in what you say and do!

Bible Story: Absalom Returns to Jerusalem
2 Samuel 14:1-21

King David's son Absalom was in trouble and couldn't come home. Joab, the king's helper, wanted to change this.

Joab sent a wise woman to the king with a made-up story. She told the king she was a widow with two sons. One son had killed the other in a fight. Now, people wanted to kill her only living son.

The king felt sorry for her and promised to protect her son. Then she cleverly said, "Why don't you bring back your own son who is away?"

The king was surprised by her words. He asked, "Did Joab tell you to say this?"

The woman answered truthfully, "Yes, my lord the king. Joab told me what to say."

Because the woman was honest when the king asked her a direct question, the king wasn't angry. He decided to bring his son Absalom home again.

Being truthful, even when it's hard, helped solve the problem!

Did You Know? Pinocchio is a famous story about a wooden puppet whose nose grows longer whenever he tells a lie! This story teaches children that others can see lies, even when we think they're hidden.

Try This:

Play the "Truth Circle" game with your friends. Sit in a circle and take turns sharing one true thing about yourself that others might not know. It could be something you like, something you've done, or something you dream about!

Ways to be truthful:

Say "I'm sorry" when you make a mistake.

Tell what really happened, even if you might get in trouble.

Don't pretend to know things you don't know.

Keep your promises.

Prayer: "Dear God, help me be truthful like the woman who spoke to the king. Help me say what is true, even when it's hard. Thank you for teaching me that telling the truth is always better than lying. Amen."

Remember: "The Lord detests lying lips, but he delights in people who are trustworthy." ~ Proverbs 12:22

Chapter 59

Understanding: Wisely Using Knowledge

Understanding means knowing why things happen or how they work. It means learning about people and ideas so you can make sense of them. It's like having a light to see what others might miss!

Bible Story: Nebuchadnezzar's Dream
Daniel 4:1-37

King Nebuchadnezzar had a scary dream. In it, he saw a huge tree that grew tall and strong. Birds lived in its branches, and animals found shade under it.

Then in the dream, an angel shouted, "Cut down the tree!" But the stump would be left with a metal band around it. The angel said the tree would become like an animal for seven years.

The king called all his wise men, but no one could tell him what the dream meant. Finally, Daniel came. God had given Daniel the gift of understanding dreams.

Daniel explained, "The tree is you, King Nebuchadnezzar. You have become very powerful. But God wants you to know that He is in charge. You will live like an animal for seven years until you learn that God rules over everyone."

Daniel begged the king to change his ways and be kind to poor people.

One year later, the king was walking on his palace roof. He boasted, "Look at this great city I built by my power!" Suddenly, a voice from heaven spoke. The king's mind changed, and he went to live with the animals, just as Daniel had said.

After seven years, Nebuchadnezzar looked up to heaven. His understanding returned, and he praised God. He learned that God is the true ruler of everything.

Did You Know? Some dolphins can understand over 100 words and commands! They're so smart they can figure out new tasks just by watching. Scientists say dolphins are one of the most understanding animals in the world.

Try This:

Make an "Understanding Box." When someone does something that confuses or upsets you, write it down on a slip of paper and put it in the box. Later, try to think of three reasons why they might have acted that way. This helps you practice understanding others!

Ways to be understanding:

Ask "Why?" when something seems strange.

Listen without interrupting.

Try to see things from another person's view.

Remember, everyone has bad days sometimes.

Prayer: "Dear God, help me be understanding like Daniel. Help me learn why things happen and how people feel. Thank you for giving me a mind that can understand your world. Amen."

Remember: "The beginning of wisdom is this: Get wisdom. Though it cost all you have, get understanding." ~ Proverbs 4:7

Chapter 60

Wisdom: The Ability to Use Knowledge to Make Sound Judgements

Wise means knowing what is right and making good choices. It means using your brain and heart together to decide what to do. It's like having a special light inside that helps you see the best path!

Bible Story: Solomon Asks for Wisdom

1 Kings 3:5-14

Young King Solomon had a big problem. He had just become king after his father, David, died, and he felt like a little child trying to do a grown-up job!

One night, God appeared to Solomon in a dream. God said, "Ask for whatever you want me to give you."

Solomon could have asked for many things - money, a long life, or power over his enemies. Instead, Solomon said, "Lord, I am young and don't know how to be a good king. Please give me a wise and understanding heart so I can tell right from wrong. I need wisdom to lead your people."

God was very pleased with Solomon's request! He said, "Because you asked for wisdom instead of riches or long life, I will give you what you asked for. You will be the wisest person who has ever lived!"

God also gave Solomon things he didn't even ask for - riches, honor, and the promise of a long life if he followed God's ways.

Solomon became famous for his wisdom. People came from faraway lands to hear him speak and ask questions. His wisdom helped him be a great king.

Did You Know? Owls are often called wise animals! While they aren't actually smarter than other birds, their big forward-facing eyes and ability to turn their heads almost all the way around make them look like they're thinking deeply about everything!

Try This:

Make a "Wisdom Journal." Each night before bed, write down one wise choice you made that day and why it was wise. Also, write down one mistake you made and what you learned from it. Wisdom grows when we learn from both our good choices AND our mistakes!

Ways to grow in wisdom:

Listen to older people who know more than you.

Think before you speak or act.

Ask questions when you don't understand.

Learn from your mistakes.

Prayer: "Dear God, please give me wisdom like you gave Solomon. Help me know what is right and have the courage to do it. Thank you for teaching me through your Word and through other wise people. Amen."

Remember: "The fear of the Lord is the beginning of wisdom." ~ Proverbs 9:10

Other Novels By Tracy Carol Taylor

Basics of Christianity

Behold, I Stand at the Door and Knock

Jesus Christ Solarpunk

Parody of Parables

Available at www.princeofpages.com

www.ingramcontent.com/pod-product-compliance
Lightning Source LLC
Chambersburg PA
CBHW040000290426
43673CB00077B/287